"Advancing the Cause of Education"

"Advancing the Cause of Education"

A History of the
Indiana State Teachers Association, 1854–2004

Indiana State Teachers Association

Purdue University Press
West Lafayette, Indiana

ISBN 1-55753-364-4

Printed in the United States of America

Library of Congress Cataloging-in-Publication Data
Advancing the cause of education : a history of the Indiana State Teachers
Association, 1854-2004 / Indiana State Teachers Association.
    p. cm.
 Includes bibliographical references and index.
 ISBN 1-55753-364-4 (casebound)
 1. Indiana State Teachers Association--History. 2. Teachers' unions--
Indiana--History. I. Indiana State Teachers Association.

 LB2844.53.U62I633 2004
 331.88'371'009772--dc22

                                 2004009050

Contents

Acknowledgments

Any endeavor that tells the story of a 150-year old organization must rely on unwavering support, tenacity, and dedication from many individuals; this was certainly true of this work. The authors wish to acknowledge the efforts, sometimes of heroic proportions, of the following groups and individuals.

The History Task Force was most diligent in their efforts to help with this book. Its membership included retired and active members of the Association, many of whom not only served on the committee but also generously allowed the authors and researchers to interview them. Our thanks go to Donita Mize, the task force chairperson, and members Mattie S. Miller, Gene Price, Dottie Short and Jack Spindler, a member who also read drafts of the manuscript. Members Sarah Borgman, John Ransford, and Robert Barcus also shared experiences and "fleshed out" the facts with personal insights.

Without Robert Barcus this project would not have reached fruition. Bob served on the task force, allowed the researchers to interview him for hours on end, answered questions on demand, found obscure documents when asked, doggedly pursued publishers, and was generally, the heart and soul of the project. He believes in ISTA and the necessity of telling its history accurately.

Oral history interviews create the weave that connects the threads of history; without these living memories, the tapestry has no color. Judith A. Briganti shared her vision for the future with the challenges facing the Association, and Warren L. Williams recalled the years of internal unrest in the mid-1980s and the concerted efforts of many to refocus the organization's energies. Robert Margraf helped illuminate how money, politics, and education were intertwined in the lives of the state's teachers in the 1970s and 1980s. Damon P. Moore, two-time president, shared his thoughts on the direction of the Association during his tenure, especially in relation to new technologies. Kathy Orison Sharp harkened back to trials and tribulations of the local teacher's association in Indianapolis after the passage of PL217. J. David Young offered his recollections as a strike leader in the early days of unionization. Even more illuminating were his insights on the relationship between the new left and unionization.

Other people, not on the formal list of narrators, talked with the authors and researchers, answering specific questions. Larry Davis was helpful in providing background on ISTA's financial crisis in the 1980s, and Garrett Harbron, the leader of the conservative faction of ISTA during the 1980s, spoke of his opposition to liberal fiscal policies.

Without the professional support of the many unsung heroes that provide the materials for the researchers' use, no book would ever be complete. The assistance of the librarians at the Indiana State Library, specifically David Lewis and Martha Wright, was invaluable. The same plaudits apply to our ISTA support from Barbara Shutters, who remembers almost everything and where it is stored, Diane Martin, who could produce two days reading material at a moment's notice, and Kathleen Berry, who made the collection of images a much easier task. And many thanks to numerous other librarians, archivists and others who located information and images.

We also wish to thank the Representative Assembly for its support.

As authors, we rely on the research, editorial and administrative support of others as well. Kelly Molloy researched early in the project, Amy Robinson provided editorial assistance, and Terri Stinson kept us, and our files and drafts, straight. Finally, we wish to thank our spouses or "significant others" for their patience putting up with us during the long days of research and in the throes of writing. This has truly been a group effort.

Weintraut & Associates Historians, Inc.

—Linda Weintraut, Ph.D.

—John P. Warner

—Connie Zeigler

Foreword

As I look out of my window in the ISTA Center and see all of the activity on the streets of Indianapolis, I can't help but be impressed with the incredible progress that our state has witnessed in my 19 years as executive director. I think about the progress Indianapolis and Indiana have made and my thoughts turn to the incredible progress that our Association has made over the past 150 years as well.

It was on December 25, 1854, that fewer than 200 educators from across the state gathered here in downtown Indianapolis to protest an Indiana Supreme Court decision that declared it illegal to use public funds for public schools. Incensed by that decision, these educators came together and formed the Indiana State Teachers Association. During the next year, members of this newly formed organization attended sessions of the General Assembly and worked tirelessly to get a bill passed that allowed the use of public funds for our public schools.

Even then, several lawsuits were filed challenging that law. It wasn't until 1883 that Indiana's public schools were finally allowed to receive public funds to operate.

Thanks to the hard work and commitment to public education of ISTA's founders and early members, public schools became the backbone of our state. And ISTA became the backbone of public education.

The Association has remained active and committed these last 150 years by elevating the teaching profession and promoting the interest of public schools. Even though our state constitution calls for "free public education," during the Civil War the Association faced the fact that some Hoosiers did not believe that a free public education was necessary. During its early years, the Association was dedicated to protecting and promoting public education and the professionalism of public school employees.

To continue that important work, in 1937 Robert H. Wyatt was hired as the organization's first executive secretary. He led the organization through the process of getting organized as a powerful influence with the General Assembly, the state universities and with other state policymakers.

With Wyatt's leadership, ISTA was influential in making significant gains for public school teachers in salaries, in working conditions and in benefits.

In the following decades, the Association worked for the creation of a collective bargaining law for teachers, improved retirement benefits and other improvements in the lives of teachers and education support professionals.

In 1972, ISTA unified with its local affiliates and with the National Education Association, giving the Association a significant presence in determining education policy locally, statewide and nationally.

Thousands of hours have been spent by dedicated members planning, preparing and publishing this anniversary edition. After 150 years, ISTA continues to be strong and serves as the largest and most visible organization that advocates for public education in Indiana. I hope you enjoy reading about the past and look forward with me to an even brighter and productive future for all school employees and the children of Indiana.

—Warren L. Williams
Executive Director

"It cannot be doubted that in the United States the instruction of the people powerfully contributes to the
support of the democratic republic and that such must
always be the case."

Alexis de Tocqueville, Democracy in America, 1863

"We just keep hammering away at this because I believe
very sincerely and without any apology that it's our job
as an organization to advance the cause of education."

Robert H. Wyatt, Oral History, 1972–75

"The mission of the Indiana State Teachers Association
is to provide the resources necessary to enable local affiliates to advocate effectively for members and for public education."

Mission Statement, Vision 2000

Introduction

"Any teacher or other active friend of education"

Shortly before Christmas 1854, David Owens of Jackson County, Indiana, journeyed to the Hoosier capital to meet with other citizens who were concerned about the state of education in Indiana. Hoosiers had cause for concern; in 1846, Indiana ranked lowest among the non-slave-holding states in the number of children attending school.[1] In fact, even though free schools were guaranteed by the state constitution, most schools in the state were "subscription," or fee-based. Even Indianapolis, the largest city in the state, did not have a "free" school until 1853.[2] Such a situation had been tolerated when Indiana was still a part of the frontier, but by 1854 the state was becoming civilized and in need of an educated citizenry to guide the course of its political and business affairs.

David Owens, a man of letters, described the first Indiana State Teachers Association meeting in a missive he penned on December 30, 1854. Owens was in town to attend the founding session of the teachers' association, but his immediate concerns were more mundane. Shortly after he and his cousin arrived in Indianapolis, they checked into a boarding-house, the former Drake Hotel, on Indiana Avenue, two blocks north of Washington Street. Taking advantage of shopping opportunities in the capital, he purchased books and gifts before making his way to the meeting that had drawn him to Indianapolis.[3]

By the time Owens reached College Hall that Christmas evening, many educators, including those who had signed the circular calling for the meeting, had gathered there already. Present were Caleb Mills, E. P. Cole, G. W. Hoss, M. M. Hobbs, Rufus Patch, and Cyrus Nutt, along with others who would affect the course of Indiana education in the coming decades. Before the end of the session, 175 "concerned citizens," including 47 "of the gentler sex," had enrolled in the Indiana State Teachers Association. According to the constitution of the Association, written by Caleb Mills, "any teacher or other active friend of education may become a member of the association by signing its constitution and if males, by paying the treasurer $1 and if females by paying 50 cents."[4]

As in years to come, presenters reminded those in attendance of their responsibility as educators. Professor Read of the State University in Bloomington gave the evening's lecture, "The Importance of the Civil Polity as a Branch of Common School Education." Read spoke of the merits of teaching civic values: "Unless the American people will make our common schools what they should be where children may be trained in their moral, social and political duties, armies and navies and myriads of population cannot save us."[5] No one who heard Read could have doubted the importance of an educated citizenry.

Over the next few days, members of the new Association attended organizational sessions, shopped, and sampled the amusements of the capital city. They debated teaching the Bible, finally passing a resolution that "the children and youth of the country be trained up in the morality of the Christian religion." They condemned book agents as "harpies . . . who flood our desks with foolish trash and silly quarrels." They listened as Horace Mann, president of Antioch College, delivered his speech on "The Duty of the State to Provide and Control the Education of Youth."[6]

In his letter of December 30, 1854, Owens wrote of the lectures and the ambience of the meetings, but the aims of ISTA were more broadly defined than he may have understood at that time. While lecturers challenged educators and affirmed the need for enlightened citizens, there was another dimension to the Association, a purposeful commitment not clearly apparent to all of those attending. Over the next century and a half, ISTA would keep education at the forefront of the agenda of the Indiana General Assembly. From the beginning, teachers and "other active friend[s] of education" energetically sought increased funding for education. Indeed, the author of ISTA's constitution, Caleb Mills, was one of the most active lobbyists in the assembly in the nineteenth century.[7]

Over the next 150 years, members of the Indiana State Teachers Association stood ever ready to advance the cause of education. This advancement was neither easy nor steady. The Association endured many crises, some financial and others organizational. Pushed at times by charismatic leaders and driven at other times by the winds of cultural change, ISTA was, and is, an organization of individuals. As such, it has been both limited and elevated by the dreams and aspirations of its leaders and members.

The history of the Association that unfolds over the following pages is varied and complex. Dates fix pivotal points in time and provide the framework for understanding the nuances of changing laws that affected the children of the state, the evolution of teaching conditions, and the ebb and flow of public concerns over the education of children. A timeline in the appendix of this book provides an overview chronology for reference.

The story of the Association falls rather neatly into three chronological periods, with the first detailing its beginnings as a loosely knit organization. This section also chronicles ISTA's quest for universal *public* education, and its efforts to establish professional standards and secure benefits for teachers. The final chapter in this section places ISTA's efforts at reform within the increasingly complex political climate of the 1920s and 1930s and examines its transition from one of volunteer leadership to one with a paid professional staff, an important organizational change that set the stage for the charismatic Robert H. Wyatt to assume the leadership of ISTA.

The second section covers the years of Wyatt's leadership, a time in which he came to personify the Association. During this era, ISTA emerged as the dominant nongovernmental force in public education in Indiana. Wyatt's directorship began as the Great Depression was ending, but his tenure was defined by an era of postwar abundance. A progressive educator, Wyatt embraced education as a means for social change. He persistently lobbied legislators for increased funding for education, including federal aid. Indeed, it was in the arena of federal aid to education that ISTA came into sharp conflict with the political and economic establishment in Indiana. Although these battles were not without cost, ISTA emerged as the most powerful lobbying association in the state by the end of the Wyatt era.

The final section looks at ISTA's transformation into a powerful union while still remaining a lobbying organization. Wyatt had laid the groundwork for the issues that shaped ISTA in the 1970s and beyond, but a new generation of advocates was destined to lead the Association. This new generation had been weaned on unionism and stirred by the rhetoric of the radicals of the 1960s. The key issues of this era were unification, collective bargaining, rebuilding, and refocusing. The closing decades of the twentieth century were marked by internal debate and self-examination as ISTA attempted to reconcile unionism, and its sometimes negative cultural connotation, with its original charge of advancing the cause of education.

ISTA has traveled far over its 150-year history, from the small group of teachers and "other active friend[s] of education" described by David Owens to a statewide federation of educators more than 48,000 strong. Members of this Association have debated the issues of education and have lobbied for their interests with a tenacity matched by few other organizations. While David Owens could not have foretold the growth and eventual power of ISTA, he certainly understood, even at that first meeting on Christmas Day, that the Indiana State Teachers Association would be a strong force for public school education.

Part One

"An Organized Body of Efficient Educators," 1854–1938

> "I know not how society can be aided more than by an organized body of efficient educators."
>
> —William M. Daily, President of ISTA, 1854

William M. Daily and the founding members of the Indiana State Teachers Association began a tradition of strong advocacy for public education, a tradition that continued for 150 years. The challenges of those first years were great. These men and women had to convince a doubtful public of the need for public education, that all children, male and female, rich and poor, and black and white, needed to be educated, and that an educated citizenry was essential to maintain and advance democratic freedoms. ISTA evolved from a loosely run but committed cadre of educators to a professional association in these first eighty-four years. This transformation was necessary for the Association to advance the cause of education for all Hoosiers.

I

"No Pinching of Economy"

At the first meeting of the newly formed Indiana State Teachers Association in 1854, its president, William M. Daily, declared, "there should be no pinching of economy in education." His audience knew there had been considerable "pinching" up to that point. The efforts of this small group of reform-minded citizens, the founders of the Indiana State Teachers Association, set in motion changes in education that would affect the way that schools were funded.[1] Along with others, these teachers were intent on petitioning the Indiana General Assembly for money to support "free," or tax-funded, public schools in order to create the educated citizenry so essential to the perpetuation of the Republic.[2]

Reform, the desire to improve what is wrong or to transform society into a better state, swept across the nation in the years preceding the Civil War. Woman's rights, temperance, and abolitionism were popular causes of the period. Reformers believed that educating male property owners—initially the only eligible voters—enabled these men to participate more fully in the democratic process. These reformers also believed that education helped women (even though they could not vote) to better nurture the next generation of responsible male citizens. In the years of the early Republic, influential and ofttimes affluent women, such as Abigail Adams (soon to be the First Lady), argued successfully that a formal education would enable women to "train [the] heroes, statesmen and philosophers" of the next generation.[3] Their advocacy resulted in the establishment of private academies for the daughters of the wealthy.

Proceeds from the sale of public lands of this new young nation provided the initial funding for public education. In 1787, the Northwest Ordinance granted land to each state within its territory to sell in support of public schools.[4] After Indiana was carved from the Northwest Territory and later made a state, its first constitution provided for a means to finance education. Profits from Section 16 in each township were designated to pay for common schools in that township. These funds quickly proved insufficient. Seeking a remedy, the Indiana General Assembly rewrote laws affecting school funding. Modifying the original plan, the assembly also allowed townships to raise funds for schools by leasing the land of Section 16 to farmers. While certainly far from perfect, according to one historian, it was "likely the number of common schools, supported by public revenue, increased as a result of these codes."[5]

In most townships, however, the state of education remained woefully inadequate. Teachers were often poorly educated and marginally qualified to teach; buildings were primitive and not well-maintained. In fact, so abysmal was this early school system that when the 1840 census was taken it showed that less than one-fourth of Indiana's school-aged children attended school. In literacy, Indiana ranked eighteenth among the twenty-eight states then in the union.[6] A decade later the situation worsened; the state's position in literacy dropped to twenty-third among the twenty-eight states, giving it the worst record among all northern states. If, as the *Indiana Common School Report* in 1848 reported, "free schools equalize conditions in society," then the need for a free, public school system in Indiana was compelling.[7]

Agitation to improve education had begun within two decades of statehood. In 1833, influential citizens in Madison, Indiana, organized the Association for the Improvement of Common Schools in Indiana. This association found that one of the greatest difficulties in forming an adequate public school system was the "want of competent teachers of good moral character and respectability."[8] Four years later, the first State Education Convention, held in Indianapolis, was attended by more than two hundred individuals who called themselves the "Friends of Common Education." The convention drew members of both political parties and representatives of most of the state's religious organizations. Governor Noah Noble served as president; Indiana Supreme Court Justice Isaac Blackford and the president of Indiana College, Andrew Wylie, were vice presidents. The group sent a "memorial" to the Indiana General Assembly requesting changes in school legislation. But their requests went unheeded. According to historian Donald Carmony, Indiana still lacked three elements key to making substantial improvements in its educational system. First, Indiana citizens did not fully believe that education was "important and desirable" for all children. Second, there was not yet a common acceptance that schools should be supported by tax money; and third, a contingent believed that it was the parents' responsibility to provide for education.[9]

Still, educators continued to push for an adequate public school system. In January 1839, another convention sent yet another request to the legislature. This time they appealed to state pride by asserting that "education was rapidly advancing in Kentucky and Ohio [but not in Indiana] because of the 'assistance . . . of an active and intelligent superintendent of Common schools.'" The constitution adopted by this convention provided for an annual meeting in order to improve education in Indiana.[10] Unfortunately, the state's financial crisis in the late 1830s, fueled by the national financial panic of 1837, nearly extinguished the efforts of reformers. Indiana educators did not reconvene until 1847.

As late as 1850, there was no state-supported school system in place. The few public common schools in existence were locally supported. Most schools were not free; parents paid small tuitions to finance "subscription" schools, or their children attended private academies. Other children, instructed by a family member or a private tutor, studied at home. There were exceptions, of course. For example, the educated elite at New Harmony, Indiana, formed its own communal school.[11] Indeed, one of New Harmony's most influential citizens, Robert Dale Owen, repeatedly spoke out for education. In 1838, he told the legislature that "we must pay for teachers or we must pay for prisons and penitentiaries."[12] The legislature proved unresponsive, prompting concerned Hoosiers to take up the cause of education.

Caleb Mills, a professor at Wabash College, launched a program of public awareness aimed at pressuring the Indiana General Assembly to institute a credible school system. Beginning in 1846, under the pseudonym "One of the People," he addressed the state legislature through a series of letters published in the *Indianapolis Journal,* a newspaper of the day. Mills's scathing critique of education in Indiana placed the blame on the legislators themselves: "Gentlemen from Jackson, Martin, Clay and Dubois counties must feel themselves very much relieved from the burden of sending newspapers and legislative documents to those whom they represent, when informed that only a fraction over one-half of their constituents can read or write." Mills's series of informative and thought-provoking letters demanded "free public schools for all the children of the State."[13] Over the next few years Mills proselytized tirelessly for major changes in the quality and funding of the state's school system.

Following Mills's second letter in 1847, the legislature passed an act to present the idea of free public schools (those supported by taxes rather than parental subscriptions) to the voters in a referendum. Up to this time many Hoosiers expressed the belief that education was not for the masses. One state legislator had, merely a decade earlier, ended a speech to the legislature with the words, "When I die, I want my epitaph written, 'Here lies an enemy to free schools.'"[14] But a referendum on public education in 1847 indicated a shift in public opinion. Fifty-five percent of those who voted answered "yes" to the question: "Are you in favor of free schools?"[15]

Still, the question of public education was far from resolved. At the constitutional convention in 1850–1851, delegates hotly debated the responsibility of the state to educate. However, the new constitution set the parameters for Indiana's public school system by fixing the Indiana General Assembly with the responsibility "to provide by law for a general and uniform system of common schools wherein tuition shall be without charge and equally open to all." The constitution also provided for an elected state superintendent of public instruction. William C. Larrabee, a mathematics professor at Asbury College, held the office first.[16]

New legislation seemed to create even more problems, however, and as Indiana entered the second half of the nineteenth century, public education legislation was mired in argument and litigation. In 1852, the

Indiana General Assembly passed a law providing for taxation by "local units" to supplement state funds distributed for tuition and to pay for building and equipping schools. Unfortunately the Indiana Supreme Court held unconstitutional the levying of taxes by township authorities, thus denying local municipalities the extra funds necessary to fully implement a system of free public education. The court decision "all but paralyzed" the new school system for the next decade.[17]

It was "out of [this] crisis" that the call arose for ISTA's formation.[18] The Association's goal was to organize for the "determined purpose of discussing the great fundamental principles of an educational system and the appropriate instrumentalities to be employed." Its membership was open to "any teacher or other active friend of education."[19] Nearly one-third of those enrolled in the convention were women, an early indicator of the importance of women in the educational profession and in this new Association.[20]

Initially, ISTA addressed issues of wages and training. The salaries of teachers were a particular concern in the poorly funded school system. Male teachers at the time earned about eighteen dollars a week; female teachers were paid only about half that amount. These salaries were less than most day laborers earned at the time.[21] While better wages for teachers was a primary concern, the membership also continued to advocate for better-prepared teachers who could educate the youth of the state in the "principles of government."[22]

Once established, the Indiana State Teachers Association met annually (or more often) to influence the course of education. In 1855, the group resolved "to labor for the establishment of [teachers'] institutes in every county in the state."[23] The resolution process, adopted by the Association early in its organizational history, enabled the membership to focus on specific educational issues during the upcoming year. ISTA's legislative committee established an early lobbying presence for public education, working with the 1855 Indiana General Assembly to amend the school laws and to provide for "a continuance of public schools" statewide.[24]

The legality of public schools, however, was still being challenged. In 1858, State Supreme Court Justice Samuel Perkins held the 1855 tax unlawful, thus essentially denying local taxation to support schools. Although some schools continued to operate through voluntary contributions, this decision resulted in the closure of many. According to historian Emma Lou Thornbrough, teachers lost their jobs and "a general exodus of trained superintendents and principals to other states" occurred after this decision. Even the state's capital saw all but one of its public schools close, throwing more than two-thirds of the city's children out of the educational system.[25]

With efforts directed toward the Civil War, progress was stalled in public education from 1861 to 1865. One educator wrote about the effects of war: "in government economy that which under ordinary circumstances is applied to the advancement and up building of education, religion etc., must now be drawn off . . . to protect the government and put down rebellion."[26] War-related activities occupied Hoosiers, and some cities' school facilities were co-opted for the war. For example, New Albany schools were closed in 1861 when the United States government rented them for the war effort.[27] Teachers were drafted or volunteered to serve in the armed forces, leaving some schools without teachers.

Despite these setbacks, public sentiment was shifting in favor of a tax-supported public education system. After the Civil War, lifestyles began to change to a mixed agricultural and urban/industrial pattern. Population and affluence increased. Indiana residents began to show concern over the state's public image outside its borders. Slowly, these factors combined to raise public support for educational reform in order to align Indiana with the most progressive states. The difficult task of changing public opinion became the mission of ISTA members; their efforts energized the legislature to fund a working system of public education and dispense with their "pinching of economy in education."

II

"A Great Awakening in Education"

The Indiana State Teachers Association fought an extended battle for its "great awakening in education."[1] Educating children in order to create a state in which people could vote intelligently and safeguard their freedoms was the prime concern for the founders of ISTA. On the eve of the Civil War, Indiana had a scattered population, leaving children in certain areas of the state with limited access to education. Schools in rural areas suffered most, although the quality of education was not particularly good anywhere in the state. Much needed to be done. For the next six decades, members of ISTA set about remedying this situation, most notably by lobbying for the creation of graded schools, improved school facilities, and universal education for all children from kindergarten-age through adolescence. However, efforts met resistance in both urban and rural areas.

In 1850, more than 95 percent of Indiana's population lived on farms or in towns with less than 2,500 inhabitants. Not until 1920 did the majority of Hoosiers live in urban areas.[2] Farm families often recognized the importance of reading and simple math, but they resisted some of the proposed educational reforms, especially any attempt to enact compulsory school attendance. Compulsory school attendance proved a hardship for these families, for farming was labor-intensive. Farmers depended on children to help at times of planting and harvesting. If children attended school during these crucial times, the family felt a direct economic impact. Farm families were not alone in opposing the strictures of compulsory school attendance, however.

The working poor and their employers in urban areas also opposed mandatory public school education. After the Civil War, as Indiana became more industrialized, emerging industries hired children as laborers, exploiting their dexterity around machinery and their ability to work in close quarters. Poor parents expected youngsters to contribute to the family income, so some of these children labored during school hours; others worked at night and slept during the day instead of attending school.[3] In 1867, the Indiana General Assembly enacted a statute limiting the length of the workday to ten hours for children under the age of sixteen working in cotton and woolen mills. Sadly even this law was not strictly enforced, and children continued to work long hours in factories.[4] For poor families, economics often superseded their desire to educate their children.

Education faced other obstacles during the second half of the nineteenth century, especially among the poor. Often children were viewed as miniature adults who ought to work rather than attend school. By the end of the nineteenth century, however, a transformation occurred; most people of the upper and middle classes came to recognize childhood as a definable period in the life cycle. Over time this view became accepted across socio-economic lines, and thus education slowly came to be viewed as necessary in preparing children for the adult world.[5]

While ideology and economic need conspired to keep many urban poor children out of the educational system in the postbellum era, rural schools faced other difficulties. Indiana law declared that local communities should bear the burden for schools through local taxation. In sparsely populated rural areas there were fewer homes and residents, and therefore fewer tax dollars in the local coffers for schools. Moreover, transporting children was a problem in rural areas, where the only school might be miles from home. Even under these difficult circumstances, rural communities continued to construct school buildings. However, many schools remained one-room, ungraded schools under the guidance of a sole teacher during the nineteenth century.[6] These ungraded schools, in which students of all ages and abilities studied together, consistently had shorter terms, less competent teachers, poorer attendance, and a more limited curriculum than their counterparts in larger towns and cities.

Urban areas started the move toward graded schools. Before the Civil War, both Evansville and Fort Wayne initiated the concept of graded schools, which grouped children by age and achievement. Abram C. Short-ridge, president of ISTA in 1868, introduced a graded system to the Indi-anapolis Public Schools and divided the grades into primary, intermediate, and high school.[7] As time progressed, other ISTA members took up the cause for graded schools, "on grounds of economy, efficiency of instruc-tion, progress in scholarship, ease of discipline, and the possibility of thor-ough superintendence."[8] In addition, graded schools allowed teachers to prepare and present their lessons more efficiently. However, graded schools came under fire by the end of the twentieth century from reformers who criticized "drillmasters," teachers who drilled students en masse rather than working with individual students.[9] Also, graded schools were impractical in rural areas, where few and far-flung students made motorized transport difficult.

Rural education continued to come under increasing scrutiny after 1876. The state superintendent of education declared small rural schools the "paramount educational problem in the state." And while many larger communities had established high schools in the years following the Civil War, in most rural areas only elementary education was available. With the majority of Indiana's students attending rural schools (as late as 1879, 72 per-cent of school enrollment was in rural townships), the need to improve them was vital. The cause was helped in 1879 with the publication of Edward Eggleston's *Hoosier Schoolmaster*, a book that did much to raise awareness of the plight of rural schools.[10] With ISTA consistently advocating for in-creased funding, conditions did improve, but slowly. By the end of the century, one commentator in the *Inland Educator,* an education periodical, referred to rural schools as "desolate and mean." He charged that they had poor ventilation, steep and winding stairs, and wells of "doubtful purity."[11]

Due in no small part to the lobbying efforts of members of ISTA, the Indiana General Assembly finally passed legislation in 1899 to consoli-date hundreds of inefficient and oftentimes unhealthy one-room school-houses.[12] The effect of this act was to bring together the resources of these small districts into larger schools with bigger budgets that could afford better-prepared teachers, improved equipment, and the space and staff to offer graded schools and secondary education.

Consolidation may have helped to upgrade the quality of teaching to some extent, but it did not solve the perennial funding problems that faced Indiana education. In 1906, the Association appointed a committee "to investigate the leaks in the school fund of the state of Indiana." Dr. Robert J. Aley was appointed chairman and his report to the membership at the 1907 convention focused on three sources of funding: the permanent fund, state tax levies, and local tax levies. The committee's conclusions were as follows: fines and forfeitures that supported the permanent fund were not being adjudged fairly; and property, normally assessed for state and local tax levies, was either not identified at all or was assessed at 30 or 40 percent of value. The result was greatly reduced funding for education. The convention heard the report, directed the committee to define the problem of low tax yields, and further directed it to report again in 1908 "in such form that the report may be carried to the legislature."[13]

The closing of one-room schoolhouses and the fight for funds notwithstanding, one segment of universal public education not addressed by government was the education of African Americans. One aspiration of the "great awakening" in public education was to create a "universal" system—one that included children of all races. Although a forward-looking document in many respects, the 1851 Indiana Constitution had made no provision to educate African Americans, of any age, even though Civil War Governor Oliver P. Morton urged such legislation, as did his successor, Conrad Baker. African Americans depended on their own resources to maintain schools.[14]

As early as the 1860s, members of ISTA resolved to make Indiana's education system free *and* "universal." During the Civil War, their commitment to educating African Americans extended beyond the borders of the state. Many teachers volunteered during the war years to teach runaway and freed slaves in Southern states. In 1864, an ISTA resolution commended the "patriotic spirit of those teachers who have given up lucrative situations and volunteered as gratuitous teachers of 'contrabands' in the Southern States."[15] ISTA members found support for their cause growing with the death of slavery.

In 1869, ISTA secured a law that gave African Americans access to a segregated public school system; eight years later a new provision to the law "allowed Negroes to attend white schools if there was no separate school available." The courts found this law unconstitutional in 1874 but it was reworded and re-instituted in 1877. In communities with large numbers of African Americans, separate schools became the rule. Separation was also the norm in most southern counties in the state, even if the number of African Americans attending school was small. Still ISTA and other public school proponents counted it a victory that Indiana now provided a free education for all children.[16]

While successfully lobbying for the institution of free universal public education and the consolidation of one-room schools, ISTA members also sought other reforms. Along with the state superintendent of public instruction and the Indiana Association of County Superintendents, ISTA pushed for greater centralization of public education in order to standardize and improve it. Members also sought a standardized curriculum in high schools that included math, science, history, English, and a foreign language.[17]

During the closing decades of the nineteenth century, members lobbied the legislature for a compulsory school attendance law. In 1897, the General Assembly passed a law requiring school attendance by all children ages eight to fourteen for twelve weeks a year. This legislation provided for truant officers to enforce the act. In conjunction with prohibitive child labor legislation enacted the same year, this law greatly increased access to an ever-improving public school system. Many children continued to work, but they also went to school.[18] ISTA also endeavored to extend the educational system to more children by introducing kindergarten education. This idea met with some resistance, however. In 1899, the General Assembly gave cities and towns the authority to establish kindergartens, but not to use public funds to do so.[19]

By 1913, Indiana's children were attending a range of schools, both public and private. In that year, ISTA secured legislation that required children to attend school until age sixteen—or, if gainfully employed, until they passed the fourth grade and were older than age fourteen. Indeed, a survey conducted by Circle of Charities that year found that most children living in Indianapolis did attend school, although working-class youngsters often went to parochial schools. These religious-based schools flourished in areas of the state with large ethnic populations. The elite continued to send their children to private schools. By 1917, Indiana ranked fourth among all the states in the number of children per one hundred enrolled in high school.[20]

In 1917, the year that the United States entered World War I, Indiana was becoming a modern industrial state. It had changed greatly since the founding of ISTA, when it had been primarily a rural state with most residents engaged in farming. Transportation routes linking Hoosiers to all areas of the United States in these decades brought new residents and new ideas and facilitated commerce. Population had increased, and industry had incubated and grown into mature businesses. Automobiles now chugged along beside horse-drawn wagons and carriages on city streets and rural roads. By the early twentieth century, four Hoosier authors, Booth Tarkington, James Whitcomb Riley, Meredith Nicholson, and George Ade, made Indiana internationally famous through their literary accomplishments and ushered in the "Golden Age of Indiana Literature." Although in this dynamic environment of demographic, industrial, and cultural growth, educators and legislators still struggled to find funds for schools and ensure an educated citizenry.[21]

Education as a whole benefited greatly from the larger cultural shift that took place in these years. A "great awakening" had occurred in public school education. No longer was the one-room log schoolhouse, with its single untrained teacher, the norm. In fact, one-room schoolhouses became an aberration as districts consolidated and staffs became professional. All children, including rural, urban, and African American, could now count a free public school education as a right. ISTA had been a primary force for this change. As progenitors of this "great awakening," the membership had educated the lawmakers and the citizens of the state on the need for improvements that brought Indiana schools into the competitive new century.

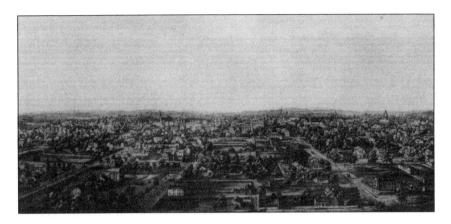

Indianapolis had been the state capital for scarcely three decades when the first meeting of the Indiana State Teachers Association convened at College Hall on Christmas Eve, 1854. Photograph by Bass Photo Company Collection, Indiana Historical Society, 314830F.

One hundred and fifty new ISTA members met the day after Christmas 1854 to elect the first officers and to listen to speakers. Indiana State Library.

In the antebellum era before the establishment of the Indiana State Teachers Association, prominent reform-minded Hoosiers, such as Governor Noah Noble, met to discuss ways to implement public education. Governors' Portraits Collection, Indiana Historical Bureau.

Robert Dale Owen, of New Harmony, Indiana, led the battle for public education in Indiana for many years. A lifelong advocate for learning and culture, he introduced a bill to establish the Smithsonian Institution while serving in the United States Congress. Photograph by Bass Photo Collection, Indiana Historical Society, 100657-F.

Caleb Mills, professor of Greek and Latin at Wabash College, effectively and tirelessly advocated for public education. He served as state superintendent of public schools in 1854 and as the fifth president of ISTA in 1859. Photograph by Bass Photo Collection, Indiana Historical Society, 224853-F.

Abram Shortridge became superintendent of Indianapolis Public Schools in 1863. Immediately thereafter he set about improving the educational system by reopening the high school, setting up graded schools, and lengthening the school term. At his insistence the capital's schools were reopened to African American children. Photo courtesy of Purdue University.

School hacks such as this one in Pendleton, Indiana, in 1908, began bringing rural youngsters to more centralized schools. Indiana State Library.

By the end of the Civil War there were 7,403 schoolhouses in the state, of which 1,100 were one-room, log structures. A decade later the state boasted 9,434 school buildings, of which only 200 were made of logs. Indiana State Library.

The funding of kindergarten became a recurring topic of debate in the Indiana General Assembly in the twentieth century, spurred on by efforts of ISTA. The children shown in this photo attended a kindergarten in Indianapolis in the 1920s, but they were atypical in that era; most children in Indiana did not receive kindergarten instruction. Indiana State Library.

Dr. James H. Smart came to Fort Wayne schools in 1865 and established a twelve-year system of instruction there. In 1873 he became the nineteenth president of the ISTA and was the first Indiana educator to serve as president of the National Education Association. ISTA Archives.

III

"A Competent Corps of Instructors"

In order to create "a competent corps of instructors," as called for by a "memorial" sent to the Indiana General Assembly in 1856, members of the Indiana State Teachers Association concentrated on issues that improved their own status, and in equal measure, the status of Indiana's public school system.[1] Members argued that in order to establish this "competent corps," better pay and retirement benefits were required. Also, ISTA wanted teachers to be well-educated and advocated various ways to elevate professional standards. Thus, the organization began a familiar pattern: striving to increase professional competence while concurrently lobbying the Indiana General Assembly for increased funds for salaries and schools to attract more capable teachers.

Education for the educators was foremost in the minds of members of ISTA. When they met in December 1855 in Madison, Indiana, they resolved to "labor for the establishment of [teachers'] institutes in every county in the state." Even though these institutes predated ISTA, the Association became one of their greatest advocates. Teachers' institutes—basically short training sessions—were conducted locally to further teachers' education and to introduce the latest in methodology. Until the establishment of Normal Schools, or teachers' colleges as they were later known, institutes were considered a stopgap measure to prepare teachers for their professional responsibilities.[2]

In 1860, ISTA members lobbied for teachers' institutes and associations to be "organized and judiciously conducted in every county." Institutes would "contribute character and influence to the teacher's profession and awaken a confidence in their behalf unknown or felt before." According to an article in the *Indiana School Journal*, institutes were "the most efficient and economic means" to improve the skills of teachers. State law mandated the conduct of county institutes, and in 1865, the county superintendents of education assumed overall responsibility for the program and appointed teachers to conduct the training sessions. Then, in 1873, the state legislature made teacher attendance at township institutes compulsory, a move promoted by ISTA.[3]

Annual conventions also kept ISTA members abreast of the latest innovations in teaching methods. When committee members found a subject particularly compelling, they would pass a resolution adopting it as worthy of ISTA members' attention. Or, if unconvinced of the subject or method's efficacy, they would resolve not to support it. For example, in 1860, they resolved that the "singing or chanting system of teaching is of secondary importance, and should only be considered an auxiliary method." In 1876, they resolved unanimously to introduce experimental instruction into the schools that would show the "nature of alcohol and its dire effects on the human system."[4]

As early as 1856, ISTA began publishing the *Indiana School Journal,* a periodical that disseminated information about education in general and the Association in particular. The first issue included minutes of the annual meeting, a question and answer section by Caleb Mills (then state superintendent of public instruction), mathematical and scientific departments, and other miscellany pertaining to teaching. As the first voice of ISTA, the *Indiana School Journal* presented the Association's views to members and others. It also educated its constituency in the latest thought on teaching practices and subjects.[5]

In 1883, the Association inaugurated the concept of teacher's reading circles. These circles, directed by ISTA, were designed to broaden the knowledge of enrollees as well as provide information for use in the classroom. Teachers who joined the circles paid twenty-five cents to engage in the prescribed course of study. In 1896, the reading material was *Guizot's History of Civilization* and *Literary Interpretations,* the latter a guide for "the principles of psychology as presented in the pedagogical studies of the past three years." By 1896, more than 13,000 of the 13,500 teachers in the state were enrolled in the teacher's reading circles. At the end of each directed course of study, teachers who passed examinations derived from reading circle materials were exempted from county licensing examinations on the subjects of science of education and literature.[6]

Examining and licensing teachers were other means employed to increase professionalism and were issues of interest to ISTA. The state required county examiners to conduct evaluations on a regularly scheduled basis to certify teachers. Certificates issued by examiners were valid only in the county in which the exam was given and, depending on the applicant's performance and record, he or she might receive either a first- or a second-grade certificate. The grades signified the teacher's level of expertise.[7] County examination dates were published in ISTA's periodical along with any qualifiers needed for attendance. For example, in 1863, the school examiner of Hendricks County announced in the *Indiana School Journal* that he was holding public examinations at Danville at 10:00 a.m. on the last Saturday of every month. Like all examiners, he required that applicants show "satisfactory evidence of moral character," although he did not specify what that evidence might be.[8]

Though supported by ISTA, teacher examinations were one area that caused conflict. ISTA wanted the county exams to be administered by teachers, not by the county superintendents or township trustees, who, many believed, inflicted personal prejudices or views on the examinees. At the annual convention in 1860, members commended the matter to the county boards of education throughout the state and strongly recommended that teachers should examine teachers. In 1863, the Hendricks County examiner made his position clear when he declared that "teachers who do not read educational journals cannot keep up with educational improvements; therefore no teacher who is not a subscriber to an educational journal will receive a certificate for a longer period than six months."[9] His word was absolute. Year after year at the annual conventions ISTA resolved to petition the General Assembly to establish qualification standards for those who supervised teachers and to gain authority for educators to license and exam-

ine teachers. In 1896, the membership asked the General Assembly to require educational qualifications for county superintendents and asked that
teacher licensing and examination be placed under the aegis of the State
Board of Education. So ingrained was the hegemony of bureaucrats that it
was only in 1923 that the Indiana General Assembly withdrew licensing
control from the province of county supervisors.[10]

Ongoing concern over the quality of Indiana teachers prompted
ISTA to promote a state college for teachers. This Normal School, as it was
called, offered more comprehensive training than the county institutes and
the annual meetings could provide. Normal schools were another means of
creating a professional, highly trained corps of instructors. In 1858, ISTA's
Committee on Normal Schools reported that the state needed one thousand "well-trained professional teachers." At that meeting the Association
passed a resolution stating that Normal Schools were "absolutely necessary"
and that ISTA should take all steps possible to hasten their opening. ISTA
was finally rewarded when the first state Normal School opened in Terre
Haute in 1870. At last Indiana was counted among the many states that
produced finely trained teachers under state supervision. In 1903, Robert J.
Aley, president of ISTA, wrote that the Normal School had three purposes: "it is a school of method, a school of new views and a school of in-
spiration."[11] These three purposes meshed seamlessly with ISTA's goals.

ISTA had more than altruism in mind as its members tirelessly
worked to improve teaching skills and to gain recognition for the teaching
profession. The organization also sought to increase pay so teachers could
earn a better living. In 1866 the average salary for male teachers in primary
schools was $32 a month; women earned only $24.80. High school teachers earned more, but still not enough. The wage for male high school teachers
was $58.40 (women $32.20) per month, but these were still relatively low
earnings.

After years of lobbying by the Association to secure increases in
teachers' salaries, in 1907, the Indiana General Assembly passed a bill providing for a sliding minimum wage based on experience, scholarship, and
other training. Now, beginning teachers were paid $450 for the nine-month
school term, while experienced teachers earned $630. This brought some
standardization to wage scales and an increase in salary for many.[12] Teachers were fond of comparing their wages to those of common laborers in-

stead of other professionals, thus punctuating their shameful pay levels. In 1924, the *Indiana Teacher* reported that hod carriers, unskilled workers in the building trades, earned 75 cents per hour, a full 20 cents more than teachers made.[13] Despite increasing levels of training and preparation and ISTA's successful advocacy for increased remuneration, wages remained low.

As members argued for living wages, they also asked for pensions and tenure for educators. As early as 1876, ISTA expressed a need for adequate teachers' pensions, but not at the expense of better wages. Teachers had an immediate need for better salaries. One writer for the *Indiana School Journal* argued, "persons are respected and have influence in proportion to their income. Let teachers be better paid and they will be more highly respected, more independent, more influential."[14] But educators also needed retirement programs. In 1907, ISTA asked the legislature for pension benefits for all teachers; however, the assembly passed legislation providing only for Indianapolis public schools to start a pension fund by levying a special tax and by assessing teachers' salaries. In 1910, ISTA lobbied for a law to provide disability benefits for teachers who had worked at least fifteen years with the membership supporting a provision for teachers with thirty-five or more years teaching experience to receive pensions. By 1915, ISTA had "secured the first in a series of teacher retirement laws" when the state created a state retirement fund administered by a state board for school systems in towns of more than twenty thousand residents. At that time, any school corporation with its own pension plan could become part of the state plan.[15] This was a significant gain for teachers in cities but did nothing to help teachers in rural areas. Finally, in 1921 a retirement law was passed for all teachers that provided for an annuity of seven hundred dollars after forty years of service.[16]

Tenure was yet another area in which teachers sought control over their professional destinies. Well into the twentieth century, job security was virtually at the whim of township trustees. The *Indiana Teacher* editorialized against self-serving trustees who cast out experienced teachers. At one school "a competent rural school teacher was let go because the trustee desired to make room on the public pay roll for his niece." Another teacher "failed of reappointment because she belonged to the wrong church." Examples such as these prompted advocates to favor tenure for its "efficiency of teaching and the welfare of the school children of the state," tying the protection of tenure to benefits for children. In 1927, the legislature finally passed a law that granted all teachers tenure after five years of service. Teachers could be dismissed if the number of jobs decreased, but they could no longer be let go on a whim or for political reasons.[17]

While members of ISTA continued to keep their own needs as workers at the forefront, much of their energy was directed at improving the school system itself. Over a number of years, educators such as Caleb Mills had tirelessly petitioned the legislature to create a good, free public school system for all students, and once that system was in place, its members worked tirelessly to improve the education of the state's youngsters. In order to raise the level of competency at public schools, members of ISTA fully supported measures that increased teacher proficiency—and that raised salaries, benefits, and job security. In doing so, the Association was trying to better the status of teachers both professionally and financially. As it did this, ISTA was growing into a powerful force for the improvement of the state's schools and for the teachers themselves.

The State Normal School was built in Terre Haute after that city donated $50,000 and a plot of land (the site of the old county seminary) on which to erect the school. Growth was slow at first but within ten years, it averaged about 300 students a term. Martin Collection, Indiana Historical Society, 378636.

ISTA housed its "part time" headquarters at the Claypool Hotel in 1922. Within two years, ISTA called the Lincoln Hotel home. Photograph by Bass Photo Collection, Indiana Historical Society, 204198-F.

One of the main criticisms of schools in rural areas was that they tended to hire teachers with less training than those in urban areas. Hence, students did not receive the same quality of education as those in urban areas. Indiana State Library.

Until 1923 teachers in Indiana were licensed at the county rather than the state level. This system gave the local units of government nearly complete control of education. Indiana State Library.

This Teacher's State Certificate was awarded to Charlotte Henderson in 1923, the first year that the state gained authority to license and examine teachers. ISTA Archives.

Robert Aley, president of ISTA in 1909, also served as president of the National Education Association and president of Butler University. Butler University Archives.

In 1914, Belle O'Hair of Indianapolis asked the Association to go on record in favor of equal suffrage, which it did with a "rising vote." O'Hair was a prominent force in education, serving on the board of ISTA and as president of the State Federation of Teachers. ISTA Archives.

Many working class parents preferred their children learn useful skills to prepare them for post-school life. Photograph by Bass Photo Collection, Indiana Historical Society, 16616.

To many teachers, it likely seemed that President Franklin Roosevelt's New Deal was for everyone but them. Indiana State Library.

"Is this the New Deal for Teachers?"

Governor Paul V. McNutt signed the Gross Income Tax bill, a "save the schools" measure, in March 1933. Looking on are (left to right) state representatives Frank Finney, Marc G. Waggener, and Edward H. Stein; state superintendent of public instruction, George Cole; ISTA executive secretary C. O. Williams; Lieutenant Governor Clifford Townsend; Robert Houghham from the Indiana Teachers Retirement fund; and state senators Anderson Ketchum and Ward Biddle. ISTA Archives.

IV

Be It Resolved

The decades between the two world wars tested the resolve of ISTA as members struggled to build upon past achievements during difficult times. Following the Roaring Twenties, a decade marked by affluence and conflict, the nation was plunged into the Great Depression. As in the past, members continued to advance the cause of education with efforts focused on reducing the power of the township trustee system. They also sought to eliminate all one-room rural schools, which they believed were inadequately preparing students to meet the challenges of the modern world. Resolutions adopted at annual conventions advocated better school facilities, increased pay and benefits for educators, a more equalized system of school funding, and consolidation of schools in the hopes of improving education. In the midst of such advocacy, ISTA began the transformation from an association administered by volunteers to one with a paid professional staff.

This era, not unlike the one that witnessed the beginning of ISTA, was punctuated by reform. The fruits of progressivism, a belief that science and government could be the instruments of good, were ripening. Through consistent advocacy women gained the right to vote, and temperance forces marshaled the passage of the short-lived Prohibition Amendment to the Constitution. At settlement houses, work continued to help the poor and new immigrants, and once more, reformers became powerful advocates for the welfare of children.

In Indiana, the reality of the state's educational system stood in stark contrast to new, optimistic progressive theories of education. While some private schools experimented with John Dewey's theories of the individual development of the child, most public schools retained their teacher-centered formal instruction. The era was marked by the need to scientifically measure proficiency. People debated the best teaching techniques, and urban schools initiated classes in manual arts education.[1] Even those who did not accept new theories began to realize that children were, indeed, the "Nation's Last Reserve" and deserving of the scientific attention paid to other groups. However, true to form, Indiana's legislature was glacially slow in funding educational reforms.[2]

A progressive experiment in Indiana education was a topic at ISTA's annual convention in 1909. William A. Wirt, a local school superintendent in Bluffton, Indiana, at the turn of the century, had instituted a "platoon" system of classes. In this system classes were rotated with recreation. Then in 1907, Wirt took his ideas to the new industrial city of Gary, where he created an entirely new school system. Wirt's plan, sometimes called the work-study-play system, has brought all ages—from kindergarten to high school—together in the same building. All areas of the school facility were utilized at all times, with one group attending classes, another receiving manual training, and still another enjoying playtime in the gymnasium or on the playground. Wirt received renown and effusive praise for his efforts from John Dewey and other progressive reformers.[3] However, his system was not widely followed in Indiana. Reform would have to come in other ways.

In 1920, Indiana's Department of Public Instruction responded to a national study conducted by a New York foundation. This study showed that Indiana ranked seventeenth among states in quality of education. The Department of Public Instruction called for a statewide effort to raise Indiana's schools from seventeenth to first place. To address this crisis, State Superintendent of Public Instruction L. N. Hines organized a series of conferences and meetings across the state to marshal support to raise Indiana's ranking. Responding to the "public attention . . . directed to the low rating of the Indiana school system," the Indiana General Assembly instructed the governor to appoint a commission to study and evaluate the state of public education in Indiana. Published in 1923, that report served as the basis of debate on public education.[4]

According to the report, a primary deficit in Indiana public education was the condition of the many small rural schools that dotted the Indiana countryside. In 1922, there were still 4,500 one-teacher schools in rural areas across the state. As one noted historian summarized conditions, the commission found these schools to be "bastions of backwardness." The commissioners wrote, "City schools are not as good as they should be . . . rural schools are much worse."[5]

A recently instituted achievement test showed that these conclusions were well founded. Pupils in one-teacher township schools had significantly lower test scores than those in city schools. The commission primarily blamed rural teachers, who, not surprisingly, were less experienced, less prepared, and for the most part, "deficient in teaching skill." Only 7 percent of these teachers had both a high school degree and at least two years of teacher training. In comparison, 52 percent of teachers in city schools could claim both qualifications.[6]

Funding was a perpetual problem for rural schools. Local property and poll taxes continued to provide approximately 90 percent of the money for schools in the 1920s. Unfortunately, rural tax rolls shrank as farmers faced an acute agricultural crisis during this decade.[7] In all cases, rural schools fared worse than those in urban areas because city schools had a denser tax base and more available funds. Yet city schools were not immune to problems.

The commission directed some criticism at administrative aspects of all schools in Indiana's system, blaming shortcomings on the poorly funded, decentralized, local school system and, in particular, the township unit. It even quoted the much-revered Caleb Mills, who had said in 1857, "It [the township unit] is nothing more than a sad blemish . . . which can not be too speedily erased from the statutes." The commission observed: "The only way to correct the defects of the trustee system is to abolish the township as the local unit." An elected county school board was the suggested solution. The commission also opined that this change in administrative level of control would reduce or eliminate the political aspects of the trustee/superintendent relationship.[8]

The commission's findings were consistent with many of the changes that ISTA and its national partner the National Education Association (NEA) had long wished to achieve. Twenty-five years earlier, the NEA's "Committee of Twelve Report" had proposed consolidation of local units into centralized schools.[9] ISTA had long been opposed to the township trustee's near total control over local schools. By law trustees had the responsibility of keeping "school buildings in good repair" and furnishing "fuel, furniture, apparatus, books . . . necessary for a systematic and proper conduct of said school." Trustees also had "hire and fire" authority over teachers and sometimes used it to further their personal ends. As early as 1915, the *Indianapolis Star* noted that teachers and principals were coming to the annual meeting that year "with the intention of wresting control of the organization from the superintendents," whom teachers viewed as the trustees' minions.[10]

The Indiana Education Survey Commission did not lay the blame for poor schools entirely at the feet of the trustees, as ISTA may have preferred, but also condemned teachers. Through many legislative efforts the Association had attempted to address the problem of inadequately prepared teachers, as in 1915, when ISTA issued a resolution calling for a professional standard that required at least one-half of the high school teachers to be graduates of a four-year college or Normal School. That resolution also proposed that county, city, and town superintendents and supervisors should have the same stringent educational requirements applied to them.[11] Members of ISTA felt that the trustees and the superintendents bore responsibility for the quality of the teaching force because they continued to hire ill-prepared instructors. As frustrating as it must have been, however, ISTA suggested that the Survey Commission's report should be received "with open minds."

Resolutions from ISTA's own annual convention in 1922 called for legislative changes in teacher training. (Resolutions developed by the assembly of educators at each annual meeting expressed the concerns of the educators and served as a guide for lobbying efforts.) That same year ISTA "urged" that the school laws of the state should be codified to protect against local misinterpretations or manipulation of the laws by the trustees and superintendents. The convention had come to recognize that the rights of teachers must be protected.[12]

Members of ISTA were among the educators who spoke out against the township unit administration of rural schools in favor of a county unit. In 1925, the editor of the *Indiana Teacher* wrote, "The control of the rural schools by trustees is an anachronism." Township trustee Edward J. Hecker wrote in the same issue: "there is no statute which can compel him [the trustee] to follow anything but his own opinion or whim." Also there was "no recourse to higher authority or any punitive measures to be taken against him [the trustee] so long as he complies with the state laws regarding the length of the school term." In 1926, ISTA also asked for the consolidation of many rural schools.[13]

ISTA found support in many corners for its positions. Former state superintendents of public instruction came out in favor of the replacement of the township with the county as the local administrative unit, as did the PTA, the Indiana County Superintendents Association, and the State Board of Education. Benjamin J. Burris, State Superintendent of Public Instruction and president of ISTA in 1924, argued that in a county unit an elected, nonpartisan school board could centralize purchasing, more efficiently use the teachers in a county, and be in a better position to levy local taxes than the township trustees.[14]

The General Assembly was not yet ready to replace the township unit with the county unit plan, however. Township trustees opposed the county unit plan, as did rural citizens, particularly Democrats. They worried that change would bring higher taxes and that local control would give way to the "city intellectuals, who do not help us in any way." Indeed, the efforts of these groups helped prevent passage of a bill to put Indiana schools under the county plan in 1923. While the county unit plan failed at this time, other recommendations were implemented. Smaller rural schools began to be consolidated into larger schools. These consolidations dramatically decreased the number of one-teacher schools from 4,500 in 1920 to only 616 by 1945. [15]

In 1923, the Indianapolis Chamber of Commerce issued a separate study that found the state's largest school system grossly inadequate. The study cited overcrowded and unsanitary buildings with few schools having indoor plumbing or electricity. In some schools, notably those with all or mostly African American students, odors from the outhouses made studying difficult; the doors of some outhouses had been nailed shut to keep children from falling through rotted flooring. The Indianapolis community demanded change, but in retrospect that change came from an unlikely source —a powerful contingent cloaked in the robes of the Ku Klux Klan.[16]

By the mid-1920s many Hoosiers were enthralled by a newly energized Ku Klux Klan. This new Klan, with its anti-Catholic, anti-immigrant, and anti-black components, was surprisingly also a strong advocate of improved education for all children. It was a vocal proponent of public education and an outspoken opponent of parochial education (which, in the Klan's view, put a foreign leader, the Pope, in control of a segment of American education). In Indianapolis, the Ku Klux Klan allied itself strongly with the Republican Party and succeeded in getting its members elected to the Indianapolis Public Schools board in 1925 on a platform that advocated an aggressive building plan, kindergarten education, and the hiring of more teachers. When the "Klan school board" was turned out in 1929, its educational innovations disappeared as well.[17]

Segregation was commonplace in education during the 1920s in some Hoosier cities. Although the construction of the all-black high school, Crispus Attucks, in Indianapolis is often tied to the rise of the Ku Klux Klan, it was planned before the Klan board took over and represented the desire of the majority of the white Indianapolis community to keep the races apart. Ultimately, Crispus Attucks, with its highly educated staff, became one of the finest public high schools in the nation. In some cities, such as Fort Wayne and South Bend, segregation occurred as a result of residential patterning. In Gary, as in Indianapolis, all-black Roosevelt High School (opened in 1931), maintained de facto segregation.[18]

In the midst of these crises, and foreseeing change, ISTA began to institute more businesslike methods of running the organization during these years. In the first decade of the twentieth century, the Association began a research program to guide its legislative lobbying. By 1914, ISTA had committed to a new plan of organization that would "form subordinate associations in thirteen districts in the state."[19] While subordinate associations were obviously needed to expand the role of ISTA, members continued to vote for an annual convention to bring together all the district organizations and members.

Although ISTA considered other locations for these annual meetings, the Association membership favored gathering in centrally located Indianapolis. Not surprisingly, the Indianapolis Chamber of Commerce actively courted the ISTA convention. The capital city profited from this annual event, which by 1921 brought 15,000 teachers to town. While in the city, ISTA members rented hotel rooms, ate at local restaurants, and shopped in downtown stores. In 1921, they resolved that at each meeting the teachers should be treated to "one high class entertainment" while in the city.[20] The city responded with enthusiasm to these conventions. Newspapers gave front-page coverage to convention activities, and local merchants felt their purses swell with profits during the days of the meetings. Although shopping and "first class entertainment" were part of the annual convention experience, ISTA members knew that their main purpose at these meetings was to develop a set of resolutions to guide activity in the coming year.

In these years ISTA become a more professional organization. A volunteer staff could no longer efficiently run its programs and publications. In 1921, ISTA created its first paid professional staff position, the office of field secretary, to "look after educational interests," publications, and other "matters connected with schools in general." Members resolved the next year to locate "part time" headquarters at the Claypool Hotel.[21] In 1924, members of ISTA's executive committee decided that it was now time for the directorship to become a full-time position.[22]

Forty-eight-year-old Charles O. Williams became the first full-time director. A seasoned veteran of the Hoosier educational system, Williams had attended Fountain City schools and had graduated from Valparaiso University before entering teaching. He also had studied law and had become a member of the Kentucky and Indiana bar associations. He worked first as a teacher in a rural school, then taught high school, and then became a superintendent before taking the position at ISTA.[23] Few understood the challenges of Indiana's schools better than Williams.

As the Roaring Twenties ground to a halt, ISTA placed "problems of taxation" at the top of its list of issues to address. Given the current crises in agriculture and rural funding of education, it also wanted to seek a way to "provide a more equitable distribution of the tax burden." Miss Clara Rathfon, ISTA president in 1932, called for teachers to "help shape public opinion . . . to the point it will demand that the outgrown tax system of Indiana be changed." Especially in these difficult times, as the Great

Depression settled on Indiana, it was important to keep money flowing into the school system.[24]

Monies were scarce for all government functions. In 1932, Indiana elected a charismatic new governor, Paul V. McNutt, who immediately began working to quell the economic crisis. On the national level, Americans selected Franklin D. Roosevelt as president, in no small part because of his optimism in the midst of overwhelming economic stress. A few days after Roosevelt assumed office Prohibition was repealed, returning money spent on policing the black market in alcohol back into the economy. It was a symbolic change in attitude, designed by Roosevelt to bolster spirits that sagged with the deepening depression.

The Great Depression brought years of uncertainty for teachers. Students who could not find jobs tended to remain in school longer than ever before, increasing the rolls in high schools and further straining already strained budgets. Moreover, the number of school days increased in this era, which meant that teachers were teaching more students longer, sometimes for less pay. In 1933, in a bow to the economic realities of the day, the General Assembly repealed the 1927 teacher tenure law for the smaller township schools. This placed the jobs of rural teachers in jeopardy. At ISTA's annual meeting in 1934 the 16,000 members present decided to unite to prevent changes that might decrease state revenue payments to local units by up to $600 per teacher.[25]

Even with belt tightening, state government made attempts to address the plight of education. With local property and poll taxes decreasing, funding from the state increased after 1933. This change came about due to the unified lobbying of farmers and teachers.[26] From a gross state income tax, Governor McNutt raised state support of schools from less than 10 percent to greater than 30 percent of all funds. That same year, the Indiana General Assembly passed the State School Relief Act, which gave more aid to poorer school districts.[27] This meant that Indiana was one of only three states nationwide to keep the doors of all of its schools open in 1934.[28] One of the major gains for ISTA occurred as the Great Depression peaked in 1937. A new teacher retirement law raised the annuity from $900 to $960 and lowered the required years of service from 40 to 35.[29]

Teachers of ISTA greeted these incremental changes with editorials calling for united action. Williams called for "unity" in order to withstand the pressures of the Great Depression. He told teachers, "We are now facing one of the greatest crises in the history of public education. . . . In union there is strength."[30] ISTA urged teachers to join the National Education Association. At a time when few teachers had extra funds for such membership, Williams issued a plea that members not cancel their ISTA membership: "Can't every teacher in Indiana give at least one day's pay as dues?"[31]

The *Indiana Teacher* also lobbied for federal involvement in the educational system. "The New Deal has been dealt to industry, labor, and agriculture, but it has not as yet reached the schools," grumbled the periodical, for teachers were left outside of the Social Security Act in 1935.[32] Indeed, editorials in the *Indiana Teacher* set the stage for the thrust of ISTA for decades to come; the Association became a vocal advocate for federal aid to education.

In 1938, ISTA suffered a blow when its long-time executive director died of a heart attack. The economic hardships of the Great Depression had made his years at ISTA difficult, but Williams had endeavored to create a united professional association and had raised ISTA's visibility within the state. During his career, he had worked to protect teachers' interests by serving on the board of the Indiana State Teachers' Retirement Fund and, for many years, as its president.[33] He had also been prominent in the National Education Association as the Indiana director since 1930 and even had run for its presidency in 1938.[34]

These interwar years had tested the resolve of ISTA. The organization emerged from this turbulent era battle-tested, if not always the victor, and poised for an era of dramatic growth. In this process, members decided that the time had come to build a more professional organization. And, after the death of Williams, the executive committee began looking for a strong and focused individual to lead them out of the Great Depression. ISTA found this person in Robert H. Wyatt.

Part Two

The Wyatt Organization, 1938–1971

> "One of the major goals of the profession should be the complete organization, national, state, and local. Until this is achieved neither teaching, nor any other work will attain the coordination and unity of purpose that should characterize a great profession."
>
> —Robert H. Wyatt, 1936

No individual, past or present, has equaled Robert H. Wyatt's impact on the Indiana State Teachers Association. He came to ISTA as the second professional director, or executive secretary, as his position was called at the time, with a set of goals that over the course of thirty years he worked doggedly to achieve. In doing so, Wyatt transformed ISTA from *one* of the associations that influenced the course of education in Indiana into *the* association that did so. At the end of his tenure, ISTA had a position as a lobby that was unmatched in the state, and Wyatt was Mr. ISTA. His persona defined the organization.

V

"The Task of Leadership"

Robert H. Wyatt announced his growing belief that "the task of leadership must be undertaken by the organized profession in a larger way" in his annual report to the membership in 1939.[1] A strong leader at a pivotal time, Wyatt molded ISTA into one of the most powerful lobbying organizations in the state and a leader in educational circles. When Wyatt joined the Association as executive secretary, he inherited a 16,343-member organization staffed by two secretaries in a one-room office in the Lincoln Hotel. Thirty years later, the membership had more than tripled, the staff had grown to 21 professionals and 51 clerical workers, and the Association was located in its own building in the heart of the Hoosier capital.[2] This transformation was accomplished through organized effort under Wyatt's guidance.

Although Wyatt was only thirty-four years old when he became executive secretary of ISTA, he brought eighteen years of experience in education to the job. Something of a prodigy, Wyatt graduated high school at age sixteen, and, after taking a summer course in teaching, became a teacher the following fall. By the time he was twenty-one, he had taught for three years and had completed a master's degree at Indiana University. In 1931, at the age of twenty-seven, he was elected president of the Fort Wayne

Teachers Association, and four years later became president of the Indiana State Federation of Public School Teachers, later called the Indiana Classroom Teachers Association (ICTA).[3] At the time Wyatt became executive secretary of ISTA in 1938, it was "in great disarray," a situation that Wyatt immediately set about changing.[4] However, his first year of leading the Association was difficult, as the country was caught in the lingering grips of the decade-long Great Depression.

Life for many, especially the poor and those in rural areas, likely seemed bleak and discouraging in 1938. Adding to the uncertainty of the times were stories that filled American newspapers of the rise of totalitarian regimes in Europe. Soon it was evident that someone had to stop Hitler's army from taking all of Europe, and, with Great Britain's declaration of war in September 1939, the United States began gearing up for the inevitable. After the Japanese bombed Pearl Harbor on December 7, 1941, the focus of the nation was on war.

World War II changed the context of ISTA's efforts. Students engaged in bond rallies and scrap drives to support the war effort. Some enlisted and left school before graduation. The *Indianapolis Star* made note of the "changes in curricular attitudes" occasioned by the outbreak of hostilities, and ISTA urged teachers "to be alert in recognizing influences that create an atmosphere in which totalitarianism lives and thrives." At a time when federal and local governments expected 100 percent commitment to the war effort in both mind and deed, anything less raised questions about one's patriotism. Yet, at the annual ISTA convention, the resolutions committee recommended the adoption of a permanent platform that included the "responsibility for presenting all points of view in the classroom."[5] Thus, ISTA promoted tolerance for opposing views even in a time of intense nationalism.

The war profoundly affected the teaching profession, however. Not just students, but teachers, both men and women, left to serve in the armed forces or to work in industry. A full 16 percent of teachers in Indiana left their positions, and many would not return to the profession. At the same time, schools in communities with defense industries experienced a rapid increase in enrollment as workers in the new factories brought their families to these areas. This migration to the industrial centers in Indiana further exacerbated the problems of a wartime-induced teacher shortage in many large cities. So severe was the dearth of teachers that, by the end of the war, ISTA set up a scholarship fund to "encourage young people to enter the teaching profession," and it established a placement service to match teachers with available positions. The problem of too few teachers with too many students was compounded by a shortage of funds for schools as money went first to defense efforts. In some rural areas schools that had survived the depression closed during the war due to financial shortfalls.[6]

Even with the attention of the nation and the teaching profession focused on the war effort, ISTA made gains for teachers through lobbying efforts in the Indiana General Assembly. Laws concerning minimum salaries, textbook adoption, and teacher retirement funds passed in 1943. One new law provided a guaranteed $125 per month for beginning teachers for an eight-month school term with an incremental increase of $2.50 per month for each year of teaching experience. Each local school corporation was responsible for any salary above that minimum. The law also set specific standards for more pay for experience and longevity, and it established different schedules for elementary and high school teachers.[7]

In 1945, Wyatt drafted a bill aimed at reorganizing the state board of education. The proposed board would have three commissions with six people on each, with the state superintendent of public instruction chairing each of the commissions. This new board structure responded to two long-time concerns of ISTA. First, it created a textbook commission to administer a new multiple adoption textbook law that provided school systems with choices in textbooks from state-approved lists. Second, this law also changed the composition of the teacher training and licensing commission to include "a minimum of four (4) persons actively employed in the schools of Indiana." In other words, professional teachers, not bureaucrats alone, were now in control of teacher licensing.[8] That ISTA made these gains was testament to the power of its lobby.

ISTA's efforts in the immediate postwar era were helped by the fact that Wyatt's wife, Margaret, served as a Republican representative in the Indiana General Assembly. During her first session, Margaret Wyatt and Earl Utterback from Howard County introduced a bill to pay for kindergarten from state monies in the same manner that grades one through twelve were funded. However, this bill never made it out of the education committee. In the next session, circumstances changed; Margaret Wyatt, as a member of the education committee, helped ISTA receive a hearing on the bills that it introduced. This prompted Robert Wyatt to introduce his first school reorganization bill in 1947, which proposed to change the township system of school government to a countywide system. The bill did not pass, but ISTA continued to seek school reorganization for the next dozen years.[9]

The Wyatts formed a powerful team, he as a lobbyist and she as a state representative. Robert and Margaret Wyatt often entertained senators and representatives in their suite at the Lincoln Hotel. He later told an interviewer that this atmosphere was better than committee meetings for conducting business because it created an "opportunity to discuss matters in a leisurely atmosphere without being in contact with the news media."[10] One legislator, Frank T. Millis, found Robert Wyatt "a very efficient operator" but "not too popular," while another, Robert P. O'Bannon (the late Governor Frank O'Bannon's father), recalled Wyatt as "a great guy." Whatever the opinion of legislators concerning Wyatt's personality, all agreed he was very successful at lobbying for ISTA.[11]

Many of ISTA's gains in the Indiana General Assembly were a testament to the efforts of its research department. In 1940, Wyatt hired Burley Bechdolt, a large, robust man known for his command of figures, to direct the research service. The service was established to provide facts and figures about education to teachers, legislators, and the public, and to keep educators informed on current education legislation. By 1946, the research service was publishing *School Law,* a series that provided professionals with the text of the laws, and *Legislative Analysis,* a series that analyzed these laws for teachers.[12] The importance of Bechdolt's efforts cannot be understated; he, and later his staff, are credited with providing the accurate and timely statistical information used to underpin ISTA's efforts at educational reform. The availability and reliability of the data, in turn, bolstered ISTA's stature in the Indiana General Assembly and strengthened its lobby.

By the end of 1945, it was clear that Indiana's schools had suffered greatly during the war years. In Indianapolis, when the city's mayor set up a commission to begin planning for the postwar world, education was part of that plan. The state Chamber of Commerce issued missives to its members calling for reforms to increase the pay of teachers in rural schools to the level of that of city schoolteachers.[13] To the membership of ISTA, Wyatt pointed out that many school buildings were inadequate: one-third were more than fifty years old and too small for projected increases in school population. He felt that the teaching profession needed to be ready to meet the needs of the more than 130,000 additional pupils that he estimated would enter schools between 1947 and 1952. While it was clear that Hoosier schools were out of date, according to ISTA's official publication, the *Indiana Teacher*, a more basic problem was the "outmoded system of school administration in Indiana that retards the achievement of better administered and better conducted schools."[14] ISTA wanted to end the township trustee's control over the education system.

ISTA, through its legislative services arm, assumed a leadership role in assessing the quality of Indiana's schools by supervising a study of the public school system. In 1947, members at the annual convention authorized the executive committee to create and finance the Indiana School Study Commission. Headed by Bechdolt of ISTA's research service, this commission was comprised of 190 people serving on seven committees and numerous subcommittees. They examined all aspects of the state's public schools, from financing to daily operations.[15]

The results of the Indiana School Study later helped guide much of ISTA's legislative activity. For example, in an effort to address funding inequalities, in 1949 ISTA introduced the School Finance Act, which set up a uniform basis of distributing state funds while still recognizing the disparate needs of individual school systems. The act also instituted a nine-month school term and authorized the reduction of class size from thirty-five to thirty students. Subsequent legislative sessions continued to use the information generated by the School Study Commission as the basis for legislation.[16]

During this period Wyatt made another organizational change, adding an office of field service. In August 1944, he established this office to serve as a public relations department and hired Borden R. Purcell to head it. Purcell's job was to interpret "the aims, accomplishments, and the problems of the public schools of Indiana to the people" and to "[enlist] public approval and support." Purcell also served as editor of ISTA's journal, the *Indiana Teacher*. Then Purcell took on the added responsibility of heading the placement service, which aided not only the individual teacher, but also the profession as a whole by helping to steady salaries. Both teachers seeking new jobs and school systems with vacancies registered with the placement service. Once a match was found, the teacher paid ISTA a fee, which was less than that charged by traditional placement services. Within three years of its establishment, sixteen hundred teachers registered with the placement service, which generated revenues of more than $8,000 for ISTA in 1948 alone.[17]

Through the Wyatt years, the staff of ISTA continued to grow. Lavonne Ramsey and William E. Franklin were hired as assistants to Bechdolt in research. New legal counseling services were established. Purcell began directing professional services in the 1950s and conducting leadership conferences. With this new assignment, he could no longer manage the two services he had previously directed. ISTA hired a new editor for the *Indiana Teacher*, and Ann Cummins continued Purcell's work in the placement service. Taimi Lahti became director of local services in charge of local conferences of classroom teachers and the promotion of "local organizations."[18]

Wyatt made these changes to ensure that ISTA was the dominant professional association for teachers in the state. To this end, he worked to unite various teacher organizations. One of his first goals was to bring the four regional organizations "back into the fold." During the Great Depression, the superintendents had divided ISTA into five geographical areas, with each area having its own meetings, boards, and dues. ISTA had become, in effect, the teachers' association of just central Indiana, but this was not to continue. Wyatt shrewdly worked out a deal with the leadership of these regional associations: ISTA would "refund to them one dollar per member" (of their member's two-dollar annual dues) if it was allowed to conduct their October conventions. This arrangement continued for many years and strengthened ISTA's position among teachers.[19] Then in 1950, ISTA and ICTA held their first joint leadership conference in French Lick. Attended by more than one hundred local leaders from all over the state, the leadership conference included workshops on school legislation, finance, public relations, and salary goals.[20] This was a giant step toward greater unity in the teaching profession.

When teachers gathered at ISTA's annual convention in October in Indianapolis, it was a newsworthy event for the city. In 1953, more than 17,000 teachers attended this gathering. At convention time, newspapers reported changes in ISTA's leadership and listed the speakers and the top-ics of their lectures. Indianapolis citizens could not fail to be aware that the convention was in town and that education was an important issue. The capital city's five radio stations and its lone television station broadcast the convention that year. [21] It was at these conventions and through the *Indiana Teacher* that the staff of ISTA kept the membership informed of the organization's goals, its activities on behalf of teachers, and its legislative gains.

In 1950, a new constitution was adopted at the annual meeting that changed the convention format for the rest of the twentieth century. ISTA's membership decided to switch from a direct assembly to a representative assembly of delegates. For the first time in 1951, delegates from all areas of the state met in Indianapolis for the business session instead of attending business meetings in South Bend, Gary, Fort Wayne, and Evansville as well as Indianapolis. Since ISTA was an association of individuals, delegates were not representatives of local teachers associations, but rather were chosen by each superintendent or college president with more than fifteen on his staff. All members of the association were invited to attend the Representative Assembly, or RA as it came to be called, but only those who were delegates could vote on "business and the election of officers." The RA was identified as "ISTA's new venture in democratic self-govern-ment."[22]

As Wyatt consolidated ISTA's position, he realized the organization needed a more visible presence in the capital city. The Association had grown, new departments had been established, and staff had increased. It was no longer appropriate or adequate for the headquarters of such a prominent Association to be located in a downtown hotel.[23] In a city that had seen virtually no new construction in the previous twenty-five years, the announcement of the construction of the new ISTA Center was big news.

Wyatt and the executive committee purchased property for the headquarters in the heart of the state and its capital city. The new building was to be nine stories tall and measure 68 by 127 feet. It would house all staff and functions of ISTA and was planned to be a center of educational associations. Wyatt himself said, "It is desirable that the program and ide-als of the Association find tangible and visible expression in such a struc-ture."[24] This new, prominent ISTA Center would stand in view of the state-house. The placement was both symbolic and practical.

Wyatt and the executive committee set about financing the building through various initiatives. First, they asked teachers to contribute. Then they began selling bonds with a "pay-as-you-go" plan in which local school systems deducted a portion of the bond cost from the teachers' paychecks. One plan called for a series "E" bond at a purchase price of $135 that matured in ten years at $200. Another plan set five payments of $13.50 each for a bond that matured at $100 in ten years. ISTA also encouraged teachers to transfer their savings to these new higher-yielding bonds in order to finance $300,000 of the project's $3 million price tag.[25]

Even with these various initiatives, the debt of the ISTA Center became burdensome. In 1963, ISTA asked its members for an increase in dues, a temporary "assessment" to pay off the building. Wyatt believed that an assessment, which was to be paid in five-dollar increments over eleven years, was necessary to ease the financial squeeze. Although the Representative Assembly tabled the dues increase that year, it did pass a vote of confidence for Wyatt. It was hard not to be supportive of Wyatt; that same year he was elected president of NEA, making Indiana's organization even more visible and powerful nationally. The following year delegates approved a $5 increase in yearly dues to pay off the construction debt.[26]

Within twenty years Robert Wyatt had effectively transformed ISTA into a recognized force in education, as well as the professional leader in education issues in Indiana. It was to ISTA that people turned for facts and figures about the state of education or to find a qualified teacher. Wyatt had established an organization that was visible and reliable in providing this help. He had also made ISTA a prominent physical presence in the city—its new modern headquarters stood in the heart of the Hoosier capital within sight of the Capitol. Under Wyatt's guidance, ISTA took up "the task of leadership" quite effectively.

The ISTA Center

On October 24, the first day of sessions for the annual meeting in 1957, members of the Association laid the cornerstone for the new ISTA headquarters in downtown Indianapolis. In doing so, they ushered in a period when the organization would be not only a presence to be reckoned with in the legislature, but also a dominant physical presence across the street from the statehouse.

The sleek, modern-looking building was completed in two years. Designed by the local firm of McQuire and Shook (the firm that designed the remarkably similar looking NEA headquarters) and built by General Contractor Colvin and Colvin, the new structure provided approximately 85,000 square feet of downtown office space. Two-thirds of the space was to be rented and one-third occupied by ISTA. At the time of opening, the Press Club occupied the top floor and Miller's Restaurant the bottom. The street-side walls were constructed of aluminum, porcelain-clad steel, and glass. The state-of-the-art building included amenities such as air conditioning and a television system. Wyatt optimistically opined that ISTA would have no trouble renting offices in such a beautiful structure at such a prime location.[27]

In 1958, delegates to the ISTA convention witnessed the official dedication of the new $3 million ISTA headquarters building. Afterward they listened to newscaster David Brinkley at the opening session of the gathering. Brinkley's partner in the NBC evening news broadcasts, Chet Huntley, was the closing speaker the following night.[28] The Association now had a building to make its members proud, a building that symbolized to the whole state the increasing stature of ISTA.

VI

Drawing Fire

The years following World War II saw Robert H. Wyatt and ISTA grow in stature as he became more and more outspoken against local political control of education and in favor of federal support of education. Wyatt's increased visibility in the public arena, along with a growing lobbying presence in the Indiana General Assembly, brought the Association under fire in the 1950s. At issue was the role of the federal government in local matters: who should or would pay for (and control) public education—local, state, or the federal government? This debate really cut to the essence of how Hoosiers viewed the world, especially government influence in their day-to-day lives. The Association's support of federal aid to education, a liberal stance in this time, pitted it against many of the conservative powers in Indianapolis and Indiana. During the 1950s in the midst of the cold war, Hoosiers—and the rest of the nation—became embroiled in a debate over the meaning of Americanism, socialism, and communism. ISTA found itself caught up in that debate.

The subject of federal aid to education first arose just prior to World War II. Wyatt later said that his interest resulted from the difficulties he encountered while seeking education funding during the war.[1] However, federal aid to education had been controversial as early as the 1941 teachers' convention, which had been held six weeks before Pearl Harbor. When a resolution supporting a combination of federal, state, and local funds was proposed, a Muncie teacher charged that "everything done by the Federal government seems to be taking something away from the people." Even though the resolution in favor of federal aid faced "vigorous opposition," it was finally adopted.[2]

Understanding the context of the times is crucial to understanding why the issue of federal aid was so politically charged. The 1949 publication of George Orwell's novel *1984*, with its "Big Brother" imagery, gave expression to the worries of many Americans in the postwar era about a strong central government. Hoosier conservatives saw any initiative of the federal government to provide money for a local matter as a move toward a more centralized government. Conservatives, both Democrats and Republicans, had endured the New Deal as a way to stem the economic decline of the 1930s, but once prosperity returned, they wanted an end to New Deal policies and federal involvement in local and state life. The Indiana General Assembly had made its position clear, for in the postwar era it proudly rejected all sorts of federal aid aimed at revitalizing the economy and infrastructure of the state. The assembly resolved that it "wanted our government to come home. We are fed up with [the] subsidies, doles and paternalism" of the federal government.[3] Business leaders concurred and talked about wanting to halt the "slide to socialism" by rejecting federal aid. In Indiana, business had always taken a strong stance against collectivism, and for more than thirty years, these interests had spoken out against the three "isms"—unionism, socialism, and communism.[4]

The wars abroad had increased sensitivity to such issues. American men and women had died to preserve freedoms. With the end of World War II, citizens continued to worry about totalitarian and socialist governments that used young people to advance their own ideology. After the United States became involved in the Korean Conflict, concerns about communism heightened; people feared both the communists at the gates and those who lived in their midst.[5] In such a charged environment, changes in funding that shifted power from the local to the national government were perceived by some as un-American. For others who did not share these fears, federal aid was a means to better public education; herein lay the source of the battle for control of Indiana education in the 1950s.

The division intensified with rising expectations accompanying the affluence of the era and with the demographic surge of the "baby boom." As the winds of the Cold War swirled, J. Edgar Hoover reminded Congress and the nation that the United States had to be ever vigilant in the area of education: the young must be protected from indoctrination by forces on the left, which promoted internationalism at the expense of patriotism.[6] This was an environment in which some worked to ferret out radicals in education, others placed renewed emphasis on the role of children in perpetuating the heritage of America, while still others emphasized the role of inquiry and the value of presenting various points of view to America's children. This last group was generally known as "progressive educators." Progressive education, based originally on the concept of change, now had come to encompass inquiry as a methodology and to stress a child-centered environment focused on teaching social skills as desired goals. Key to progressive theory, however, was the idea that government could be the instrument of some good.[7]

The campaign for state superintendent of public instruction in 1950 reflected some of the prevailing tension concerning education in Indiana and foreshadowed some of the debates of the coming decade. Using the *Indiana Teacher* as a political stump, Wilbur Young, the Republican candidate, and Deane E. Walker, the Democratic candidate, appealed to ISTA's membership for support. Young, who had risen through the ranks from a classroom teacher to local school administrator to assistant state superintendent of public instruction, wrote, "Realizing that our liberty and freedom are being undermined by subversive Communistic forces both from within and without, I pledge . . . my most vigorous efforts to help you meet this menacing challenge."[8] Walker, the incumbent state superintendent, who had "been engaged actively in educational work for 38 years," took a different posture. "In education lies our ultimate hope of defeating the false foreign ideologies which now threaten our freedoms. Teachers have become America's first line of defense. Our burden is a heavy one."[9] Wilbur Young won the election in a national Republican sweep at the polls.[10] The consequences of the Cold War were being felt in public education.

Public education came under increasing scrutiny in 1951, especially "progressive education." For example, the National Council for American Education, a group of physicians with members in Indiana, initiated a campaign against teachers. Its literature charged, "Literally thousands of teachers are continually propagandizing for socialized medicine and all other socialist tenets."[11] As a member of the National Education Association Legislative Commission in 1951 and 1952, Wyatt devoted "a considerable amount of time in efforts to enact federal aid to education." He viewed the National Council for American Education's endeavor with increasing concern and warned: "The danger to the philosophy of public education from these anti-public education organizations cannot be over estimated, for they are the advance guard in what may be the major battle of the twentieth century: the battle for the minds of men."[12] It was a "battle for the minds" of children, not men, that was unfolding in education.

Pasadena, California, was another nexus in the debate over progressive education. William Goslin had gone to Pasadena in 1948 to become the superintendent of its progressive school system. The school system was in trouble, however. It faced problems associated with blending a new minority population with the old, predominantly white one, teachers who wanted depression-era salary cuts revoked, and a need for additional school buildings. Goslin attracted critics quickly, especially from the majority community, who opposed the increased costs of education and who were interested in seeing traditional values taught in the classroom. According to Arthur Zilversmit, author of *Changing Schools: Progressive Education Theory and Practice, 1930–1960*, for some it became the equivalent of a "religious crusade" to restore traditional values and to oppose what they perceived as Goslin's radicalism.[13] Goslin lost his job. The result of this "crusade" concerned some educators in Indiana, and naturally, as the leader of the largest teachers association in the state, it was Wyatt's responsibility to address these concerns. Wyatt's public remarks in favor of free inquiry and against those attacking public education, of course, drew fire.[14]

The Pasadena case was hotly debated not only by teachers but also by the public at large. The *Indianapolis Star* criticized Wyatt for his support of free inquiry and his refusal to be stampeded into anti-communist statements. Two of Indianapolis's main newspapers, the *Star* and the *News,* owned by the conservative Eugene Pulliam, became increasingly critical of public education in general and of Wyatt and the *Indiana Teacher* in particular. The editors at the *Star* charged that the periodical published "several articles by outsiders containing highly colored and propagandistic charges" from people who "want to destroy our democratic system."[15]

Then in 1952, the United States Supreme Court upheld the Feinberg Law. This 1949 New York law provided for the dismissal of teachers who were members of subversive groups, who taught subversive ideas, or who refused to answer questions put to them by investigative committees.[16] The *Indiana Teacher* labeled the Supreme Court's decision of "significance to teachers everywhere" and ran both the majority and dissenting opinions in its April 1952 issue.[17] From the tone of the *Indiana Teacher*, it was clear that the leadership of ISTA worried about these excesses of vigilance and their effect on public education.

That same week the newly created Indiana Textbook Commission declined to endorse Frank Magruder's *American Government.* Magruder's text, a standard in civics courses for thirty years, had been banned recently in other school systems across the United States.[18] In order to remove the Magruder text from the list of recommended books in Indiana, several groups, including the Chamber of Commerce, parent teacher groups, and veteran groups, charged that it was "pink tinged"—a familiar pejorative of the anti-communist era. John Burkhart, the parent of a student at Shortridge High School, said that even though the textbook had been revised, it "still had some socialistic passages. Any book having such a notorious history should not be adopted."[19]

That year State Senator Floyd Stevens, a former township trustee and the head of the senate education committee, verbally attacked Wyatt by insinuating that the ISTA director had socialist leanings. Township trustees had a long-standing adversarial relationship with ISTA. The approximately 1,100 trustees, locally elected from each township in Indiana, exercised enormous power on education and local and state political decisions.[20] Thus, when Stevens spoke before members of the Indiana Township Trustees Association, he was speaking to a powerful lobby. He charged that the 1948 study sponsored by ISTA, "An Evaluation of Indiana Public Schools," also had been "pink-tinged." Stevens further alleged that ISTA had "blacklisted him" because he was opposed to federal aid to schools and that Wyatt supported the Pasadena educator "fired for having Communist connections." However, when Wyatt suggested that such statements could be interpreted as slander, Stevens muted his accusations and said that he was not challenging ISTA's patriotism.[21]

Ever combative, Wyatt did not back down from the position that he had taken on the sanctity of academic freedom. In October 1952, ISTA invited two men to speak on a panel, even though, according to William Book, executive director of the Indianapolis Chamber of Commerce, both men had connections to the Socialist Party. It must be noted that Book was one of the staunchest critics of federal aid of all sorts. During the 1930s Book had served as director of the Emergency Relief Administration and during that tenure developed a lifelong aversion to federal aid. But while Book may have led the opposition to federal involvement, he was not alone in his fight. Ideology placed Book and others in the business community at odds with Wyatt, who continued his call for federal aid to education. ISTA's stance also was at variance with a portion of Indiana's parents. In 1952, the Indiana P-TA Members Study Group attracted attention by mailing survey letters to all teachers, hoping to confirm that ISTA's position on federal aid was not indicative of the feeling of all teachers.[22]

ISTA wisely remained aloof from one incident that claimed national attention. The incident, which illuminated the educational climate of the era, also revealed the depth of conservatism regarding education in Indiana. Mrs. Thomas White, a member of the state textbook commission, spoke out in opposition to books and authors that she felt had a communist agenda. She specifically targeted *Robin Hood*, a book that she said promoted un-American values. Dubbing the book "red bait," she charged that it as well as any references to pacifist Quakers should be eliminated from the school curriculum. Then in 1955, Mrs. White made national news when she called for a ban on books written by John Steinbeck and Eleanor Roosevelt.[23]

In the midst of these red-baiting allegations, an investigation of another sort was directed at ISTA's finances. Under the leadership of Wyatt, ISTA had developed a reputation as an association with considerable lobbying powers. In 1953, the office of the secretary of state initiated an inquiry into ISTA's lobbying efforts. A discrepancy was noted between a financial expenditure on a report turned in by Wyatt shortly after the legislative session ended and a report later submitted by ISTA's Legislative and Professional Welfare Committee. Wyatt, with the approval of the ISTA executive committee, refused to provide Secretary of State Crawford Parker with the supporting records of the Association that Parker demanded. The *Indianapolis Times* wryly noted that the secretary of state was playing with "political dynamite." His office had no authority to subpoena records and after a flurry of activity in the press, the matter was dropped.[24]

Soon thereafter, ISTA held its one hundredth convention in October 1953 and began preparations for a yearlong centennial celebration in 1954. According to the *Indiana Teacher*, "ISTA's Just Bustin' Out All Over ... with nationally known speakers and top notch entertainment."[25] During 1954 people looked to the past and found that many of the organization's original concerns over power, public education policy, and funding remained unresolved after one hundred years. Other issues, regarding the role of educators in society, had taken on an increasingly hard edge.

In the year in which Senator Joseph McCarthy held hearings to ferret out communists, delegates to ISTA's Representative Assembly spoke of patriotism, the role of schools in perpetuating the American way of life, and their concern for the protection of the rights of individual teachers, especially in the face of ongoing Congressional investigations. The membership of ISTA recognized the threat of communism: "Our country is in the gravest danger of any time in its peacetime history," but it also acknowledged the importance of free inquiry. The *Star* was stirred not by the words of the resolutions and speeches of that hundredth convention, but by what it saw as a dangerous spirit. Its editorials charged that "ISTA has given the false impression to parents and schoolchildren" that the McCarthy hearings "gravely threaten the survival of American freedoms."[26]

ISTA paraded its role in Hoosier history during its centennial celebration in 1954. The festivities at the Indiana State Fairgrounds Coliseum began with Governor George N. Craig vowing to fight for higher salaries for teachers. Following was a pageant written by Chelsea S. Stewart about the first one hundred years of ISTA. Twenty-two members of the Indianapolis Symphony Orchestra provided the musical background for the production. In the finale, 252 teachers carrying red, white, and blue parasols formed the American flag. Who could doubt the teachers' patriotism?[27]

Education became a prime national concern in 1957 as Russians launched the first satellite, *Sputnik*. Admiral Hyman Rickover, a critic of progressive education, blamed the school system and its lack of rigorous standards in math and science for the United States' failure to be the first to launch a satellite into space. The president of Harvard called for more money devoted to education. *Why Johnnie Can't Read—and What You Can Do About It* became a national best seller.[28] Raising educational standards became a central issue among the general public and educators.

Preparing students "for tomorrow's world" was the theme of the 1959 teachers' conventions held in seven Indiana cities. Teachers recognized that bright students needed to be challenged, but also that all children needed to be educated, including the "slow learners, the retarded, the emotionally disturbed . . . the physically handicapped . . . [and] youngsters with social or economic problems," those whom educators were coming to acknowledge as "exceptional children." By offering sessions on how to deal with these children, ISTA was leading the way in preparing a new generation of educators.[29]

The 1950s also saw a shift in the legal parameters of segregation of schools. In 1954, the United States Supreme Court decision in the anti-segregation case of *Brown v. The Board of Education of Topeka, Kansas* negated *Plessy v. Ferguson*, an 1896 ruling that had allowed racially "separate but equal" schools. Under pressure from its minority communities, Indiana had already passed a law in 1949 to desegregate its schools slowly, beginning with kindergarten. However, since few schools actually had kindergarten, compliance was poor. Then in September 1957, federal courts ordered the desegregation of Central High School in Little Rock, Arkansas, which brought federal troops to the school. The *Indianapolis Star* went on record saying that Indiana had to end segregation in order to prevent federal intervention, but it would be many years before the state addressed the issue of desegregation.[30]

During the 1950s ISTA and Robert Wyatt remained at odds with many in the business community. While many conservative public servants cried for a return to local government and its reliance on local funding for education, Wyatt very likely did not consider the "strings attached to federal aid" a problem for teachers; he just wanted money to upgrade the educational system. Wyatt, a longtime supporter and active member of the

NEA, knew that any educational initiatives or money coming from the federal government would have some NEA concerns attached to them. However, the philosophically liberal Wyatt and the conservative Indiana General Assembly wouldn't reach a meeting of the minds on this issue until the 1960s when Hoosier lawmakers muted their objections to federal aid.

The years of debate over the communist threat had wrought great changes in ISTA. In the past, most press coverage had been positive. The Association had been considered benign, composed of "school marms and masters" who met once a year in the capital city to discuss educational issues and who quietly lobbied for increased salaries and better schools. The "biennial battle," the struggle for power in the Indiana General Assembly between the township trustees and teachers, had been intense, but was gradually being won by ISTA. Power was shifting from local units; this put ISTA under fire for its "liberal nature" as it squared off against the political "organization" in Indiana.

Federal Aid to Education

In an interview conducted in 1975 after Robert H. Wyatt had retired, he recalled his battles over federal aid to education while serving as president of the National Education Association: *My interest in federal aid to education began somewhere around 1945 or a little before, primarily as a result of the effects of the war* [World War II] *on the schools. . . . We came to the end of the war with the schools seriously deteriorating. In 1943 this became evident and the National Education Association, which has for probably fifty years been in favor of federal aid to education, introduced a bill in the Senate, which became the subject of enormous battles and bitterness.*

The whole matter of federal aid to education revolved around two issues, the religious issue and the economic issue. The chief opponents of the bill were the United States Chamber of Commerce, the National Association of Manufacturers, and in many respects, the Catholic Church. . . .The big successful battles on federal aid came beginning in '61 and '62 in the Kennedy Administration and followed on through the Johnson Administration.

Indeed, as president of the NEA, Wyatt went to the White House to discuss the federal aid to education bill with John F. Kennedy: *It was a very beautiful sunny afternoon, November 19, 1963. . . . We went down to the White House about four o'clock. Mrs. Wyatt was with me. Dr. Carr and I went to the president's office and the president said to me, "Whom do you have out there?" I said, "The executive secretaries of the states and they are very interested in hearing from you. We've got the vocational [education] bill through both houses and the higher education bill through both houses, both of them in the conference committees and it appears that there are only details to be ironed out before final passages." The president said, "What do they want to hear?" I said, "They want to hear you say that next year we're going to pass federal aid for elementary and secondary education."*

Wyatt remembered being so *horribly shocked* over Kennedy's assassination only three days later that he had to pull his car to the side of the road to *get my equilibrium.*[31] It was not until 1965 that President Lyndon Johnson signed the Elementary and Secondary Education Act into law.[32]

In 1925, as school districts all over the state began new construction, Wabash built its new high school. This school had four units: a main building, a gymnasium, an auditorium, and a vocational building. Photo by Needham's Studio, Wabash, Indiana.

A young Robert H. Wyatt became executive secretary of the Indiana State Teachers Association in 1938. Indiana State Library.

When Wyatt took over as executive secretary of ISTA, its base of operations was the Lincoln Hotel. Photograph by Bass Photo Collection, Indiana Historical Society, 128984.

Schools such as this one in Knox County typified the township school overseen by the township trustees in the 1940s. Indiana State Library.

At the outset of World War II, the *Indiana Teacher* featured patriotic covers as both teachers and students left for military service. ISTA Archives.

ISTA promoted the idea of teachers purchasing bonds to pay for the new ISTA Center. Photo by Marie Fraser, *The Indiana Teacher,* ISTA Archives.

ISTA chose a site directly across from the Statehouse as the location for its new headquarters. ISTA Archives.

Grace Pennington as Miss ISTA was pleading for help from a banker "villain." Carroll Phillips, who portrayed the banker, was seeking a high rate of interest to finance the building of the ISTA center. Tom Jett and Roger Greenwatt stood ready to rescue her from the banker's evil throes. ISTA Archives.

Ed Cotton, president of the Press Club, signed a contract for space at ISTA Center as Robert Wyatt, ISTA executive secretary, Ed Cotton, Frank Salzarulo, and Paul Schick, members of the Press Club board of directors watched in July 1957. Photo by William A. Oates, *Indianapolis Star.*

The ISTA Center was completed in 1958. ISTA Archives.

While Robert Wyatt and ISTA drew fire from many in the community, he and the members of ISTA stood together. In 1958, past presidents of ISTA gathered for a photo with Robert Wyatt. Seated (left to right) are: Glade Rohrer, R. E. Hood, H. L. Smith, W. E. Wilson, and Ralph Tirey. Standing (left to right) are: Robert Houghham, Thelma Ballard, Albert Free, Margaret Sweeney, Rose Boggs, K. V. Ammerman, and Wyatt. ISTA Archives.

Gains were made for teachers in the early 1960s at the state level. Robert Harris (right), president of Indiana Retired Teachers Association and Robert H. Wyatt (left), executive director of Indiana State Teachers Association, look on while Governor Matthew E. Welsh signed three teacher retirement bills in March 1961. *Indiana Teacher* photo.

John F. Kennedy spoke to educators in the Rose Garden at the White House in November 1963, just days before his assassination. On his right is Robert Wyatt, who was president of NEA that year. NEA photo.

Wyatt was "Mr. ISTA" during his tenure. No other person before or after had as much power and presence as he had in the organization. ISTA Archives.

Robert Wyatt's legendary influence on the General Assembly was lampooned many times in political cartoons. ISTA Archives.

Birch Bayh understood the power of the teachers to elect politicians. In 1968, he made it a point to be at Cadle Tabernacle to greet Hoosier teachers. ISTA Archives.

Thelma Spannbauer (left), president of ISTA in 1968, shared a moment with (left to right) Joanna Hock, Harold Negley, and Ronald Jensen. ISTA Archives.

Arnold Spilly conducted his first news conference as acting director on 3 May 1971. Many thought that he would be chosen executive director by the board of directors. ISTA Archives.

VII

"The Top Political Party"

When Mrs. Harriet Stout lost her bid for reelection to the Indiana House of Representatives in 1958, she blamed the "top political party in the state"—ISTA. The decades of the 1950s and 1960s saw ISTA's power and influence in politics increase markedly. The Association supported candidates "friendly to education" and targeted those that it considered "unfriendly." In addition, ISTA continued its well-established practice of marshaling political support for its educational issues and drafting legislation to send to its "friends" to introduce in the legislature. The Association's reach was extensive, and under the directorship of Robert H. Wyatt, it used its strength to push its agenda through the Indiana General Assembly and to elect politicians who supported its causes.

Stout, like other political candidates, learned how far the arm of ISTA reached. Somewhat illogically, she charged that the shortage of teachers facing Indiana schools was the fault of ISTA rather than due to the record numbers of baby-boom children entering the educational system. She called for additional people to be licensed to teach and wanted licensing requirements lowered to accomplish this goal. Her opponent, Democrat Earl Utterback, a teacher in Kokomo, noted that only seven other states required fewer courses in teaching methods than Indiana to license a teacher, implying that the licensing requirements ought to be raised, not lowered. Consistent with progressive educational theory, Utterback said that teachers "must know the child as well as the subject" to teach effectively. At the same time, Stout also attacked the lobbying efforts of teachers in the General Assembly. In a position not likely to increase her popularity with ISTA, she stated that teachers should not be paid for days spent lobbying for funding of educational issues at the statehouse, even if they took sick days or personal days to do it. Stout's antipathy toward ISTA may be attributed to her belief that the Association had contributed to her defeat, but it also illustrated her misunderstanding of educational issues and lack of concern for issues dear to teachers.[1]

The savvy Wyatt understood that the collective voice of the teachers could sway elections. In the 1950s, political candidates were not just listening to what ISTA members said, they were addressing those members on their home ground, at the annual convention. For example, both Harold Handley and Ralph Tucker, candidates for governor, spoke at the annual meeting in 1956. Wyatt expressed his appreciation of Handley's efforts as lieutenant governor in the *Indiana Teacher*, praising him and other legislators for "great contributions" and for devoting "endless hours to the task of working out school programs."[2] How much weight Wyatt's words carried in the general election cannot be known, but Handley became the next governor of Indiana in 1957.

Whether or not ISTA could win an election for a given candidate can probably never be documented. However, candidates other than Stout claimed that ISTA caused them to lose elections. In 1958, ISTA distributed a leaflet showing the procedure for voting a split ticket. Wyatt noted that the Democratic platform "implies support" of issues he considered important to ISTA. Robert P. O'Bannon, a Democratic state senator, was a great supporter of education and a fan of Wyatt as a lobbyist.[3]

Wyatt *was* an effective lobbyist. He and his wife moved into the Lincoln Hotel for the duration of the legislative session to be closer to the action, and he made a point of becoming acquainted with every legislator, often meeting with them in small groups. The charismatic Wyatt paid attention to detail and was ever careful to acknowledge those who helped advance ISTA's legislative agenda; one legislator recalled receiving 3,500 thank you letters from teachers after he sponsored a bill for Wyatt. Few lobbyists could match that effect. Wyatt's efficacy also came from his understanding of the school-funding formula, as well as the data generated by the research service. Besides this internal fact gathering, Wyatt depended on his far-flung network of information sources (school superintendents) for information used to argue in favor of ISTA initiatives. His avowed opponents could not match this information-gathering capability in these years before databases and computers.[4]

As ISTA's power in the General Assembly increased, the phrase "salary schedule" became a mantra, with ISTA asking each successive legislature for increases in the wages of beginning teachers and for incremental raises to the wages of experienced teachers. In 1952, Wyatt told the *Indianapolis Star* that anything less than a $3,000 salary for beginning teachers and a $6,000 salary for educators with master's degrees "would be an insult to the profession of teaching." Wyatt did not pull these numbers out of the air; they were wages that would place schoolteachers squarely in the middle class, a socioeconomic standing that, by the mid-1950s, was defined by a family income of $3,000 to $10,000. By 1957, Wyatt was asking the General Assembly for salary schedules that began at $5,000; at the time the average starting salary was $2,994 in township schools and $3,775 in larger cities.[5]

With the increased number of students entering Indiana's schools, the state faced two crises: a dearth of qualified teachers and inadequate school buildings. In 1954, Wyatt predicted that 2,767 teachers would be needed to teach the growing legions of students. ISTA also predicted that the state would need 1,350 new classrooms. In many areas local property taxes were not adequate to pay for such construction, and the General Assembly began considering state aid for these schools, a move that was opposed by some, including the Indiana Chamber of Commerce and the *Muncie Star*.[6]

During ISTA's annual convention in 1958, Wyatt's "tub thumping," in the words of the *Indianapolis Star*, for increased state and federal financing of schools came into conflict with his former chosen candidate, Governor Harold Handley. Handley was in favor of raising the state's level of commitment to local schools, but was steadfastly against federal aid. Handley knew he traveled over shaky ground when he spoke out against ISTA's platform, so he made a preemptive attempt to bolster his standing in the eyes of the membership. He reminded the assembly, "I'm talking to you as your governor and if you've heard I'm not interested in education, you've heard wrong." Handley said the local property tax "set-up [was] outmoded, and antiquated, [and] must be revised." Wyatt reminded the group that the funds from the state had fallen to less than 30 percent of the total cost of running the schools. He called for a shift from local property taxes as the foundation of school monies to other state sources, and he asked for the state to solicit and accept federal aid. It may have sounded a vaguely threatening note to Governor Handley when Wyatt warned: "I hope we don't experience the same frustrations in the 1959 Assembly as in the past, when a few could secure key spots and thwart the wishes of many."[7]

During 1959, ISTA garnered changes in legislation that it had sought for many years. The Indiana General Assembly finally passed the School Corporation Reorganization Act (commonly called the school consolidation bill) that year. This bill consolidated many of the small township schools into larger ones. Because these county schools were administered and financed on a countywide basis, the stranglehold of the township trustee on educational matters was loosened and more funding began to come from the state.[8] However, federal funds remained a minor part of each school system's budget.

ISTA's interest in electing candidates receptive to its programs continued in the 1960s. In 1960, Philip Willkie, the son of one-time presidential candidate Wendell Willkie, was a Republican nominee for state superintendent of public instruction. Philip Willkie complained that Wyatt used the *Indiana Teacher* as a tool to promote Democratic candidates for public office. Although that year ISTA threw its support to Governor Matthew Welsh over his opponent Crawford Parker, who had called for an accounting of ISTA's funds in the 1950s, members affirmed their "political impartiality" by resolution at the annual convention in October.[9]

This alleged impartiality of ISTA apparently did not diminish its executive director's attempts to guide voting. Judge Arch N. Bobbitt lost his campaign for reelection in 1962 as the only Republican judge on the state judicial ticket. The *Indianapolis Star* reported that in June 1961 Bobbitt had declared unconstitutional a law that ISTA had lobbied through the General Assembly. The legislation would have enabled school corporations and other government units to triple their bonding power. In the case, which

ISTA pursued through the courts at the expense of $3,000 in legal fees, the justices returned a four-to-one ruling against the law. Judge Bobbitt wrote the decision and became the symbol of ISTA's defeat.[10]

Wyatt had copies of the decision "sent to all our members pointing out who had written the opinion and the effect that it would have" on education. Although Wyatt denied exerting any "personal influence" on Bobbitt's loss, he made it known that ISTA had been "greatly disappointed" in the outcome of the case. The situation became the focus of editorials in the Indianapolis newspapers. Eugene S. Pulliam, publisher of the *Indianapolis Star* and the *Indianapolis News*, spoke out against ISTA's influence, condemning Wyatt's apparent ability to "defeat a judge for interpreting the Constitution of Indiana according to his best judgment and with the support of three of the other four judges." The editor of the *Indianapolis Times*, owned by out-of-state Scripps Howard, however, defended the Association's right to vote against candidates whose views they did not endorse.[11]

It was well known that ISTA had become a powerful force in elections in Indiana. Its efforts in the political arena were a reflection of its interest in continuing to improve the status of teachers and the conditions of Hoosier schools. Electing "friendly" officials was an important step toward achieving these goals. While ISTA was advancing its status as a lobbying powerhouse, however, a movement was beginning that would influence the direction of the Association for the next thirty years.

In 1962, a group of young college students gathered in Michigan to author "an agenda for a generation"—the Port Huron Statement. The statement outlined a plan of action for the "New Left" and recognized that, while they sought the "unattainable," they did so "to avoid the unimaginable"—a continuation of the status quo. Using grassroots organizing to accomplish social aims, the New Left vowed to empower the powerless, especially the poor and blacks. Few, especially those of the Old Left, likely recognized the full import of this gathering at the time. As ISTA continued business as usual, its members could not foresee the impact that the ideology of the New Left would have on teaching. That impact would be profound, however.[12]

By the mid-1960s a new militancy was beginning to be felt as teachers began speaking out for more control over their lives and the classrooms in which they taught. In 1965, Robert Wyatt drafted a legislative proposal for a professional negotiation bill for teachers. Two years later ISTA presented the Indiana General Assembly with legislation to recognize the largest teacher's association in any community as the official negotiator for those teachers. At that time, some local teachers' associations were negotiating contracts for their members, but for the most part individual teachers negotiated their own contracts with the local school board—if there was any negotiating at all. Unwilling to embark on a reactive militant course of action to reach its goals, ISTA passed a resolution in 1968 stating it would support teacher strikes if teachers followed established procedures, such as conducting studies, seeking mediation and arbitration, and giving the school board warning of any impending strikes. (In actuality, the Association had been following this practice for some time, but it was now official policy.)

ISTA began providing support and help with contract negotiations to the local associations. In 1969, ISTA started a grassroots network of field service representatives in order to "[bring] service closer to the teacher in the classroom." Upon request, a field representative could help the locals with their contracts. In addition, ISTA also held seminars to demonstrate effective bargaining techniques, sometimes called "begging techniques," so that local associations could better negotiate with their school boards.[13] The time had come for local grassroots efforts to help the individual teacher.

At this time, three major organizations represented teachers in Indiana—IFT, ISTA, and ICTA. The IFT (Indiana Federation of Teachers), which was primarily a union rather than a professional organization, was present mostly in the northern part of the state in highly industrialized areas; it was affiliated with the AFL/CIO. ISTA was an organization of individuals, but it also had "affiliated" organizations. In 1968, affiliated associations of ISTA were the Indiana Classroom Teachers Association, Indiana Association of Junior and Senior High School Principals, Indiana Association of Elementary School Principals, and Indiana Association of Supervision and Curriculum Development. These affiliates were given seats on the ISTA board to create a unified effort in the legislature.[14] The third major organization, Indiana Classroom Teachers Association (ICTA), was a professional organization comprised of local associations. ICTA and ISTA were drawing closer together.

In the fall of 1968, Wyatt spoke of reconciliation and of the leadership role that educators must take "to heal social wounds." In doing so, he was reinforcing his vision of education that extended beyond just teaching the "3 Rs" within the confines of the classroom. It had been a year of turmoil as the grassroots efforts of the New Left in the early 1960s had evolved into rage-filled protests. The assassinations of Martin Luther King, Jr., and Robert F. Kennedy had deeply scarred the nation, and the heretofore nonviolent resistance had turned violent. As young people were burning draft cards to protest the war in Vietnam, Wyatt lamented that "into and through this greatest social conflict of the century, schools must find their way."[15]

These were difficult years for schools—and for ISTA. The General Assembly refused to increase expenditures for schools. In the fall of 1968, Thelma W. Spannbauer, president of ISTA, spoke of the frustration of teachers and their resulting "militancy." She issued a warning that "teachers no longer are willing to take crumbs from the community table." Again and again Wyatt expressed "frustration" with the salaries of teachers, especially in 1967 after the Indiana General Assembly imposed a tax rate ceiling, which put schools in a financial bind. The *Indianapolis Star* reported that ISTA's Representative Assembly (RA) "approved whatever militant actions the ISTA leadership may deem necessary to get more tax funds for public schools."[16]

In 1969, ISTA made a dramatic show of power. An estimated 15,000 teachers clogged traffic on 86th Street in Indianapolis en route to a teachers' meeting at North Central High School's gymnasium to endorse ISTA's demand for the state to double funding for education. Wyatt called the meeting to protest stalled talks over the budget. The strong response by the teachers resulted in the closure of many schools later in the week and moved the legislators to appropriate more funds for schools.[17] The incident dramatized the power ISTA had at its command and lent credence to its appellation as the "top political party."

Despite this accomplishment, Wyatt's annual message in the fall of 1969 was steeped in bitterness. It was a year that he credited with "hard-won victories," but also a year of increased dissent within the Association. In the past, Wyatt and his staff had exercised such control over the budget that they had not presented it to the executive committee (later called the board of directors) or to the RA. That year, when Wyatt heard rumors that certain members were maneuvering behind the scenes to demand to see the budget, he preempted them by presenting the budget to the executive committee and then to the RA. According to Robert Barcus, "Bob [Wyatt] had confided in us ahead of time, he said, 'We'll just take care of the sons of bitches. . . . If they want to see it [the budget], fine.'" Wyatt printed enough copies for every member of the RA and had it ready when questions arose. Then he said, 'Jesus Christ, if you want to see [the budget] . . . there it is.'" In hindsight Barcus felt that Wyatt's anger was not based on any hidden aspects of the budget, but rather "he thought the board and the RA were micromanaging the organization."[18] The RA was challenging Wyatt's autonomy over day-to-day operations. This was a sign of change within ISTA.

Wyatt's way of running the organization was coming to an end. In 1969 he lost two trusted lieutenants, Burley Bechdolt and Borden R. Purcell, who retired that year.[19] His time-tested methods of garnering support for ISTA through a gentlemanly application of influence on "friends of education" were becoming outdated. As the 1960s drew to a close, Wyatt's control of the process of change both inside and outside the organization was being wrested from his hands. Teachers, who were bent on gaining increased control of their profession, demanded a greater voice in their state association. Some local teacher organizations were negotiating with local school boards and in some cases they were winning. ISTA, long a professional organization for individuals, had to change in order to remain viable in the late 1960s. Sensing this shift, Wyatt decided to leave the organization he had led for almost forty years.

In no small part due to Wyatt's lobbying abilities, ISTA wielded considerable power in the 1950s through the 1970s and had become a de facto political party, considered by many to be one of the most powerful lobbying organizations in the state. Its influence could make or break a political candidate's bid for office; legislators courted the Association. Robert H. Wyatt led ISTA through the first tentative steps toward teacher negotiation, but the rate of change within ISTA and its ability to accommodate a more activist population of teachers far outstripped the capacity of ISTA's aging leader. Wyatt saw the future, helped prepare ISTA for it, then realized he would have no part in it.

The Missing Retirement Funds

In 1970, Robert H. Wyatt called for "militant action" by members to ensure that "missing" money was returned to the teachers' retirement fund. This "militant action" included filing suit against the state of Indiana for money withheld from the teachers' retirement fund. Retirement pay was a major part of their "benefit" package negotiated at contract time. In fact, Wyatt estimated the retirement package's worth to each individual teacher at $100 a month, no small amount in 1970.[20]

ISTA had taken up the cause of pensions in the nineteenth century and had secured legislation with its first retirement law in the early twentieth century. In 1921, the Indiana General Assembly established a state board to oversee these funds, and then in 1925 executive secretary C. O. Williams first served on that board.[21] Since that time, ISTA's executive director had been a member of the board, often its president.[22]

The problem began when two governors withheld the money that the Indiana General Assembly appropriated for the retirement fund in order to balance the state budget in the 1960s. According to Wyatt, during the years that Roger Branigan was in office this amounted to more than $10 million, and during Edgar Whitcomb's tenure more than $16 million was withheld. None of this was illegal; state law allowed the governor to reduce an agency's expenditures to keep the budget of the state balanced.[23] However, Wyatt charged that these actions placed the future of older teachers in jeopardy. So ISTA filed suit to have the funds returned. In reprisal, Whitcomb removed Wyatt from the Indiana State Retirement Fund Board. Further controversy arose when the governor's office raised questions concerning the investments of the State Retirement Fund, perhaps to obscure the main question: When would the money be returned?

Then in 1971, Wyatt's personal pension became controversial. He returned the pension payments that he had been receiving since 1955 for his years of teaching, plus accrued interest. This allowed him to qualify for the larger pension he had lobbied through the Indiana General Assembly. Even though he was now eligible to receive as much as $17,828 a year, he opted to take a monthly installment of $1,000. While his activity was legal under the letter of the law, it was an opportunity for his adversaries to criticize him, especially because most retired teachers received less than $2,400 a year.[24]

These incidents combined to draw attention to the need for reliable, reputable investors, to the responsibility of the state not to short-change the fund, and to inequalities in the system of funding the retirement of teachers. ISTA was able to secure the return of the money and Wyatt retired with his $12,000 a year pension, but this was not the end of the matter. Teachers were forced to sue again in 1984 to have another $30 million returned. They won this suit as well, but retirement funds have remained a source of ongoing concern.[25]

Part Three

The New Advocacy, 1971–2004

> "The mission of the Indiana State Teachers Association is to provide the resources necessary to enable local affiliates to advocate effectively for members and for public education."
>
> —Mission Statement, *Vision 2000*

The Indiana State Teachers Association began a transformation in the early 1970s from a professional lobbying organization of individual members to a statewide union of local teacher associations. Collective bargaining, teachers' rights, working conditions, and, of course, salaries dominated ISTA's agenda in these years. Lobbying continued to be an important function of the Association, but no longer was it personified in the executive director; instead it was a function of local political action committees. ISTA was still a "powerhouse at the statehouse," but its organizational focus and means of achieving its goals radically changed with its new advocacy. In fact, this new advocacy changed the face of education in Indiana.

VIII

Teacher Unity

The 1970s was a decade of change. Within the framework of a national movement toward participatory democracy and militant grassroots advocacy, teachers demanded more control over their profession, their association, and their workplace. The most dramatic change for the Indiana State Teachers Association came with Robert H. Wyatt's retirement in 1971. This left a void in leadership to be filled by a new executive director and, for the first time, a full-time elected president. Concurrently, the National Education Association mandated the unification of all affiliated associations across the United States, which meant that in order to maintain membership in ISTA, teachers were required to join their local association and the NEA. Finally, in 1973, the Indiana Classroom Teachers Association (ICTA) merged with ISTA, which left only the members of the Indiana Federation of Teachers (a teachers union affiliated with the AFL/CIO) outside the fold of teacher unity. These initiatives, which made ISTA the dominant teachers association in the state, came at a cost. Change brought discomfort to some members and, at times, crisis to the Association.

For many across the United States, the late 1960s and early 1970s were a time of shattered hopes and dashed promises. Record numbers of the baby boom generation entered college or were drafted to serve in Vietnam. The Vietnam War divided the nation as the meaning of duty and patriotism became subjects of debate. In 1968, the country witnessed the assassinations of civil rights leader Martin Luther King, Jr. and presidential candidate Robert F. Kennedy. The same year, police met demonstrators in the streets of downtown Chicago with tear gas and billy clubs while delegates to the Democratic National Convention conducted sessions behind concrete barriers and barbed wire to select a candidate for president. The antiwar movement grew stronger, and with the death of four student protestors in 1970 on the Kent, Ohio, campus of Kent State University, more violent. That singular event marked the end of innocence for many young people. Furthermore the civil rights movement, which had begun peacefully with the work of the Student Nonviolent Coordinating Committee and the marches of Martin Luther King Jr., turned into the militancy of Black Nationalism.[1]

ISTA began its own metamorphosis in this era with a new generation of leaders. When Wyatt retired in 1971 there was speculation that his job would go to his associate director, Arnold W. Spilly.[2] Instead, the ISTA screening committee decided by a slight margin to offer the position to "an outsider" rather than a "Wyatt man"—to break the ties with the past. Their choice, Ronald Jensen, brought ISTA a change in leadership style and substance. Unlike Wyatt's behind-the-scene machinations and discreet way of single-handedly applying pressure within the Indiana General Assembly, Jensen's goals and style (and that of ISTA in this era) were rooted in teacher activism and in unionism. He had been a member of the "Michigan Mafia," as activists from the militant Michigan Education Association (MEA) were called. (MEA had already won collective bargaining in that state.) As a result, Jensen made it clear from the outset that he considered striking "one of several means to settle an impasse."[3] He wanted his leadership as it applied to the day-to-day operations of ISTA to be different from Wyatt's. As a corollary, however, he would have to accomplish his goals with considerably less power and leverage than Wyatt had enjoyed.

At the time of Jensen's hiring, power was being realigned between the staff of ISTA and its elected leaders. Board members and the Representative Assembly (RA) now expected a greater voice in the decision-making process within the Association; they also wanted to know the details of the operation of the Association, ranging from personnel to budget.[4] The board of directors was no longer charged with just "[carrying] into effect all orders and resolutions of the Association"; now the members were to "conduct, manage, and control the affairs and business of the Association between meetings of the Assembly."[5] At the same time, the RA began meeting twice a year instead of annually. It was believed that this would allow a fuller expression of wishes and needs of the membership.[6] In later years, the story of this realignment of power from the paid staff to the membership was told and retold among members as a point of pride, acquiring an almost legendary significance.[7]

In 1972, the year that Jensen became executive director, the constitution of the Association was changed and the elected position of ISTA president became full-time. Again, this represented a shift in the balance of power. Prior to 1972, Wyatt had been the sole spokesperson of ISTA; from this point onward it was more often the president, not the executive director, who represented the Association in public. Other duties of the president were also expanded; no longer did he or she merely preside at meetings of the RA and "perform all functions of office." Now, the president was entrusted to "make appointments to committees . . . promote public relations . . . for the Association, and to assume speaking engagements," among other duties. In essence, the president had acquired the role of the organization's chief executive officer. With this added responsibility came the diminished power of the executive director. Thus, the executive director became the "chief administrator of the Association," equivalent to a chief operating officer in the corporate world.[8] In a short period of time ISTA had become a much more member-directed association.

Even though Jensen was operating with less authority than Wyatt, he told members that he expected "to do many things that have not been done before" to meet the evolving needs of ISTA.[9] One of those "many things" was to push passage of legislation to allow teachers to bargain collectively at contract negotiations. Other goals included full funding of the teachers' retirement fund and increasing the state's appropriation to the general education fund. It was no surprise that one of his "prime internal priorities" was the creation of Unified Service in Indiana; Jensen had been the "chief architect" of Michigan's UniServ program.[10]

In 1970, NEA had started the UniServ (Unified Service) program to provide local associations with a variety of legal and political services.[11] In the fall of 1972, NEA revised its constitution to include unification, which required that in order to be a member of NEA, ISTA, or any affiliated local teachers' association, a teacher had to join and pay dues to all three. No longer could teachers choose to become a member only of their local or state association. The drive for unification, which was based on a federated system of teacher organizing, was not new. It had begun in 1944 as a way to build NEA's membership and its power at the national level. While Oregon immediately adopted unification, other states were slow to follow. Indiana adopted it in the 1970s when required to do so or lose its NEA affiliation.[12] This federated model was absolutely essential for NEA's and ISTA's new union paradigm. The melding of these three associations' interests and memberships made unified action both possible and inevitable—theoretically unification and the increased membership would also enable UniServ to be a more viable service.

Unified action was costly, however, and NEA increased its dues to help pay for fielding the initial placement of UniServ offices. Then, NEA provided funds to state associations such as ISTA to help set up UniServ offices; this funding was based on a formula related to the number of Hoosier teachers who were members of both NEA and ISTA. For example, in 1975 and 1976 NEA refunded to ISTA more than $7 per member (approximately $253,000 in total) to be used for Indiana's UniServ program. By 1988, NEA was sending about $15 per member back to the state association to maintain the UniServ program. So prominent did UniServ become that its expenditures accounted for nearly 50 percent of ISTA's total budget by 1988.[13]

The services provided by unification were key to UniServ's efficacy. Its staff provided counseling in the area of teachers' rights in case of legal difficulties. Professional development was encouraged at the local, state, and national levels through the conference on instruction, in-service education conferences, leadership training conferences, workshops, and publications, including the *Teacher Advocate*, *TODAY's Education*, and *NEA Reporter*. Insurance programs were started. UniServ's personnel trained teachers in the art of negotiation strategy, the responsibilities of leadership at the local level, and public relations.[14] UniServ's directors conducted school finance workshops, provided retirement counseling, and coordinated the flow of information used in negotiations from ISTA's research bureau to the leaders of local associations. In some settings, UniServ's negotiators were active participants in the local bargaining unit and argued issues across the table during contract talks; in other locales they were less conspicuous as advisers and providers of research data to buttress local arguments for change.[15] Unification had made UniServ possible.

Unified membership, which was intended to unite teachers, also proved divisive, however. Within a year's time, ISTA lost members as some teachers rebelled against the forced membership in all three associations. A primary point of contention was the expense of paying dues to three organizations. To cover increased costs ISTA raised dues from $30 to $40 in the mid-1970s to nearly $240 by the late 1980s.[16] Although UniServ was clearly directed at helping teachers win contract negotiations with superintendents and administrators, it became a source of antagonism to the latter groups and resulted in them leaving ISTA. ISTA was becoming more participatory and democratic; classroom teachers now formed both the rank and file and led the organization.

Still the loss of superintendents, coupled with the temporary withdrawal of many teachers after unification, created a dire financial crisis within the Association. The crisis was so great that Jensen's job appeared to be in jeopardy. Nonetheless, Joanna Hock, a classroom teacher and the first full-time president, announced the extension of Jensen's contract in 1973. The board's "vote of confidence" for Jensen came, according to Hock, from their belief in Jensen's ability to guide ISTA even though its membership had dropped 30 percent.[17] However, this financial crisis was threatening the viability of the Association.

Hock later recalled that it became clear UniServ would have to be redesigned. Staff had to be reduced and districts had to be enlarged in order to keep ISTA fiscally sound. Initially, the UniServ program had divided the state into forty districts with a staff member in each district.[18] Now the number of districts in the state was trimmed to thirty-three, and UniServ as originally envisioned was scrapped. However, the new, leaner program provided essentially the same services as the old for unified teachers.[19]

Another initiative designed to achieve teacher unity was in the offing in the pivotal year of 1973. With the transformation of teachers' associations into the union model, the Indiana Classroom Teachers Association (ICTA), which had focused on professional issues, merged with ISTA. Joanna Hock, president of ISTA, noted in the *Teacher Advocate* in 1973 that the merger would assist the "two statewide organizations . . . working for teacher unity," and concentrate professional and instructional development under one umbrella organization. The merger represented a significant shift for ICTA, which had severed its relationship with ISTA in 1970 over philosophical differences.[20]

ICTA, formerly the Indiana State Federation of Public School Teachers (ISFPST), had been a long-standing presence in education in Indiana. When Belle O'Hair and other committed professionals formed ISFPST in October 1916, its mission was to "become the spokesman for classroom teachers in the Hoosier state." Since the early twentieth century, the federation had conducted sessions in October at ISTA's annual convention and for many years had its own section in the *Indiana Teacher*. The federation worked in conjunction with ISTA to influence legislators to improve the educational environment in Indiana. As one example, the federation and ISTA jointly drafted and lobbied for the teacher tenure law passed in 1927.[21] The two associations even had a leader in common; Wyatt had served as president of the ISFPST from 1935 until 1938, when he became executive secretary of ISTA.[22]

Before the merger could occur, however, the two organizations had to resolve philosophical differences. With its ties to NEA, ISTA had become more focused on teachers' rights and collective bargaining than on professional issues, the area of ICTA's primary focus. As a precursor to the merger, ISTA agreed to increase its emphasis on professional development, curriculum, and instruction. In turn, ISTA gained the tacit approval of ICTA's members for Public Law 217, the collective bargaining legislation. Ninety percent of ICTA members voted in favor of the merger.[23]

The form and function of the organizational structure of the Association changed dramatically after 1971. Classroom teachers had wrested control of the organization from paid staff; the Representative Assembly, not the executive director, guided the Association and set its agenda; and the presidency had become a full-time position. By the 1980s, the length of the president's term was extended to three years, which enabled the president to capitalize on experience and provided continuity in leadership. The president now directed the board, set the agenda, and worked with the board to develop a strategic plan for the organization. With the increased role of the RA, the standing committees, and the president, came a new role for the executive director as the person who made the vision of the collective into a reality on a daily basis.[24]

During this period, the Association found itself in the position of sometimes uncomfortable melding of what appeared on the surface to be mutually exclusive ideals. Jensen's appointment represented a shift from old-style leadership dominated by one individual to a union model, which emphasized the concept of teachers' rights and focused less on professional development. Classroom teachers who had been involved in advancing teachers' rights, the new advocates, became leaders of the Association. This caused substantial realignment in internal power relationships. In years to come the president wielded considerable power in shaping the organization's agenda and objectives. Ironically, as the association model became more democratic and allowed for more participation by the classroom teachers, membership choices became constrained with mandated unification. Finally, the merger of ICTA and ISTA in 1973 saw the professional philosophy of ICTA subsumed under ISTA's advocacy of teachers' rights. In this decade, teacher unity had been achieved, but teachers were still assessing the costs.

"A Pivotal Time"

Joanna Hock, the first full-time president of ISTA, reminisced in 2000 about her tenure: *For me the "winds of change" began in 1970 when several of us attended our first NEA/RA [National Education Association/Representative Assembly], [in] San Francisco, as local association delegates. In frustration of trying to read and keep up with the action on the floor, several delegates decided to meet as a group on our own in an attempt to make sense of the RA business. Interestingly, at least three of us from that group later became ISTA presidents!*

In the spring of 1971, [the] ISTA Board of Directors directed the executive committee to develop the proposed annual budget for the board's consideration. . . . I'm not sure who had prepared the ISTA budgets before, but I do remember vividly the executive committee's reaction as they really studied the numbers in the budget and heard the answers from the new acting executive director and the business manager to everyone's questions. This set the stage for the board of directors developing a budget to be presented to the ISTA/RA for adoption. I remember receiving a phone call from a member who demanded to know the executive director's salary. I told the caller [the salary] and added what my salary was as the full-time president. I was thanked for the direct answer. While it may have not been our intention to be secret it certainly appeared that way to our members and created another obstacle to establishing a member-voice organization.

Early in 1972 the board of directors directed the staff to develop UniServ. After many hours of discussion, debate and motions the board of directors agreed on the design of UniServ, the new service arm of ISTA. This meant also identifying UniServ districts, hiring UniServ Directors, continued discussion and training with the membership regarding everyone's role and responsibility to make this system work. The system was no sooner set up and working than ISTA leadership finally became fully aware that we were in deep financial problems. This board had "inherited" some situations not of its own making, but coupled with the new programs we added, it became imperative we make decisions based on realities! We could not afford UniServ in its present design! . . . Basically we scrapped the first UniServ system and redesigned an affordable one! This meant, however, that UniServ Districts became larger; respected UniServ Directors were cut; and membership was up in arms! As president I got many opportunities to meet local leaders and members to explain why all of this happened and how we were going to fix it!

IX

Once Organized

Reflecting on the history of collective bargaining, a member of ISTA stated, "Once organized, teachers became more effective. Bargaining is now accepted . . . and contract settlements are achieved in a respectful and professional atmosphere."[1] Such was the legacy of Public Law 217, which set forth the structure for negotiations between teachers and local school boards and finalized a move toward collective bargaining and teachers' rights that had begun in the 1940s. In the late 1960s, it had become accepted, even fashionable, to take on "the establishment." By that time a group of vocal, militant teachers had gained sufficient strength in the Association to launch a protest against the entrenched educational system bureaucracy. As a result, strikes ensued, which forced politicians and administrators to realize they could no longer conduct contract negotiations as they had in the past. Decades of cumulative frustrations over inequity, inequality, and dual standards of behavior were bringing teachers to demand collective bargaining.

The impetus to organize arose from a sense of powerlessness that some teachers experienced at contract time. Local teachers associations usually agreed to accept any pay raise, no matter how small, because they lacked the power to demand more. Don Mann, a long-time member of the Concord Teacher's Association, recalled that when the local association requested a salary increase, "the local president would hand the salary request to the board while the rest of us [the officers of the local association] stood in the back of the room. We were then told that our request would be considered and we would be informed later. So, we all went home—and waited to be informed."[2] Mann's experience was not uncommon. Other teachers complained of unprofessional treatment by local school boards and superintendents during contract negotiations. Indignities that had been silently borne in the past now contributed to the dissatisfaction and alienation that some teachers experienced.

Citizens generally held teachers in high esteem, but also expected them to adhere to high standards of conduct in their perceived role as torchbearers for children. Teachers were expected to maintain impeccable personal and professional conduct. When teachers gathered in later years, they recounted stories of not being able to visit a bar in their hometown and of being so fearful of losing their jobs that, when they imbibed at home, they buried the bottles in the yard rather than put them out in the trash. Women hid pregnancies in order to keep teaching as long as possible. In some cases, administrators warned teachers to stay out of local politics. With virtually no voice in determining the terms of their contracts, teachers also had little control over curriculum development and other education-related issues.[3]

Anger grew among teachers as school administrators continued to make decisions unilaterally and without responding to such basic issues as teachers' rights, professional responsibilities, and pay needs. It is not surprising, therefore, that in an era that gave birth to vehement antiwar protests, Black Nationalism, and bra-burning feminists, teachers began to use aggressive negotiating tactics. Public schoolteachers were using the strike to achieve their goals.

The transformation of teachers' associations into labor unions had been a long time in coming. On a national level, the first union exclusively for classroom teachers, the National Federation of Teachers, was organized in 1899. For more than fifty years, NEA and its affiliates, such as ISTA, resisted unionization. NEA had taken the position that unionizing teachers was comparable to unionizing the army: both served the state for a higher good and neither should be unionized. In addition, leadership felt that it diminished the professional image of teachers to align with workers. However, in 1960 union members associated with the AFL/CIO successfully organized New York teachers to win collective bargaining there. At that point, NEA sent a team to New York to see if it could gain recognition as the local bargaining agent for these teachers. NEA lost this battle, but it was clear that the time for teachers' unions had come. Hence, NEA switched its legal status to that of a labor union when it adopted its new constitution in 1962. That same year it drafted model collective bargaining statutes that thirty-one states later adopted.[4]

In Indiana, as elsewhere in the nation, strikes became increasingly common in the late 1960s when teachers and administrators could not come to terms in contract disputes. In 1968 alone, eight teacher strikes occurred across the state. That same year, Indiana saw the Highland Classroom Teachers Association negotiate the state's first "master" contract (one that addressed salary, benefits, and the atmosphere in which teachers worked)—a milestone in bargaining. However, Highland's success was the exception rather than the rule in Indiana in 1968. Five years later, only eighteen master contracts had been negotiated. During that same period, thirteen strikes also occurred when school boards and teachers' associations reached impasses in negotiations.[5]

One of Jensen's first priorities as executive director was to secure passage of a law that gave teachers or their representatives the right to negotiate contracts. Representatives of ISTA had mustered statewide support for Otis Bowen in his run for governor in 1972. It has been reported by some that Bowen gladly traded his future support of collective bargaining legislation for the Republican gubernatorial nomination in the next election. Not surprisingly, soon after the new governor took his oath of office, the road to collective bargaining grew smoother with Bowen's support.[6] According to some, Bowen and the Republican-dominated General Assembly realized that they faced a choice between more teacher strikes or the passage of a law that would provide a structure within which contract negotiations could be conducted in an orderly manner under controlled circumstances.[7] They chose the latter course.

In 1973, the Indiana General Assembly passed Public Law 217, the collective bargaining law for teachers.[8] PL 217 required both teachers and school boards to enter into collective bargaining, and it codified a system of redress for teachers through the Indiana Education Employee Relations Board (IEERB). Teachers now had the ability to appeal to the IEERB when they believed school boards and/or superintendents had treated them un-fairly. Though lauded as a great step forward for teachers and Indiana edu-cation, most observers expressed surprise that PL 217 had sailed smoothly through the legislature.[9]

In September 1973, just months after the governor signed PL 217 and three months before it went into effect, teachers in the Highland School District in Northern Indiana went on strike. It was an on-again/off-again strike that reached a climax in late September when the entire negotiating team for the Highland Classroom Teachers Association was jailed. The teachers contended that the school board was refusing to enter into mean-ingful negotiation on such issues as class size, grievance procedures, salary, and maternity leave. Even though PL 217 did not become effective until January 1, 1974, ISTA took the position that the Highland School Board was violating the wishes of the Indiana General Assembly by refusing to ne-gotiate. According to Ron Jensen, "the law [was passed] to forestall just such unilateral blocking of bargaining agreements."[10] The strike ended in October 1973, and ISTA filed suit on behalf of the teachers on the bargain-ing team who had lost their jobs as a result of the strike.[11]

Not all members of ISTA agreed with the confrontational tactics used in the Highland strike. In 1973, a report issued by a visiting committee of the National Council of State Education Associations noted a divergence among ISTA members, some of whom demanded "militancy" and others, the more conservative faction, who thought that ISTA was "moving too far too fast." These factions, according to the report, had brought "internal af-fairs to a boil."[12] During the Representative Assembly in October 1973, Jen-sen chided some local teachers' associations for "dragging their heels" and attempting to "go it alone" instead of following the procedures set forth by PL 217 for collective bargaining. It was clear that not everyone or every lo-cal agreed with the direction that ISTA was going.[13]

PL 217 did have an immediate impact on contract negotiations. Following passage of the law, negotiations between teachers and school boards immediately became calmer. There were fewer strikes during the five years following the passage of PL 217 than there had been in the preceding five years. In the first year after the legislation's passage, teachers in all but two school corporations in the state organized and selected an exclusive rep-resentative to handle their negotiations.[14] However, the law did not do everything that teachers had hoped, nor was it palatable to the bureaucratic structure it was meant to mitigate. In May 1974, six months after PL 217 went into effect, Jensen contended, "The worst kept secret among the teachers of Indiana is that there is a conspiracy operating among and between superintendents and school boards with regard to teacher bargaining. The evidence is mounting that the quarter-backing for the various and sundry harassment and stalling tactics [in contract negotiations] is in fact emanating from the superintendents and school boards association and their various advisers." This was not an issue to be settled easily. [15]

Teachers asked for additional legislation to protect their job security, and the Indiana School Boards Association recommended actions that administrators should take in the case of failed negotiations. "How to Deal with Teacher Strikes" was a master plan for how not to cooperate with teachers; it even advised administrators of "strike indicators."[16] Among other tips, the document suggested that administrators keep a list of substitute teachers who were willing to cross picket lines; contact local police for increased security; order employees to turn in building keys before strikes commenced; and use a Polaroid camera when photographing striking teachers. It also advised school corporations that "if you want to attack, attack the parent organization"—ISTA.[17]

As many teacher-dominated negotiating teams went to the bargaining table for the first time, they were dismayed to find that PL 217 allowed them to bargain only narrowly on salary-related issues (wages, fringe benefits, and hours). It did not allow teachers to bargain the calendar year, only the number of hours they worked per day and the total number of days covered by the contract.[18] In addition, PL 217 did not give them the right to strike. As a result, ISTA president Raymond Gran was calling for a "right to strike" law in 1978 in order to "untangle collective bargaining disputes that have left teachers in 25 Indiana school districts without contracts for the current academic year."[19]

ISTA had made a philosophical transition into a union, even to the point of adopting the jargon of other labor unions. In 1975, the *Teacher Advocate* ran a long piece by Roger Fierst, an ISTA assistant executive director, who explained why ISTA was demanding "agency shop." Long a trade union concept and supported by past union legal precedents, agency shop was called "fair share" by ISTA members. Fair share required all teachers, even non-members, to pay a service fee to the "bargaining agent."[20]

The legality of fair share was upheld in Indiana court cases, and the fees paid by members and nonmembers were used to fund contract negotiations. Fair share fees paid to ISTA in 1987 and 1988 alone amounted to $164,000; ISTA received the full amount of the fee and redistributed portions to NEA and the local associations.[21] (The exception was in the northern sections of the state, where the American Federation of Teachers, an affiliate of the AFL/CIO, continued to hold sway as the bargaining agent for the area's teachers.) Having long struggled with the concept of ISTA as a union, teachers at least accepted, if not embraced, the notion that their rights were being advanced within the context of a union paradigm by the mid-1970s.

Teachers had long wanted due process legislation as part of their legal rights in order to better protect those with tenure. While PL 217 protected teachers against blatant retribution, school boards sometimes found ways to circumvent the law by claiming dismissals were for other reasons. For example, in 1975 Dale Harris, an assistant executive director, charged that seventeen tenured teachers faced dismissal.[22] One was "an active member of the school's bargaining team" who faced termination because of a cluttered desk. Despite hours of "marathon hearings," the school board took only five minutes to reaffirm its decision to fire the teacher. According to the *Teacher Advocate,* due process in such situations would allow "fair evaluation procedures with time to rectify existing deficiencies . . . documented evidence [and] a hearing and binding decision before an impartial third party."[23]

In 1978, the first due process law, Public Law 110, was passed. In a preemptive response to PL 110, the law firm Bose McKinney & Evans wrote to its school board clients in March 1978 that "henceforth the procedure and reasons for the non-renewal of a semi-permanent teacher or teacher who is in their third year of teaching will be much more difficult. As a consequence, now is the time to act." In other words, now was the time to fire teachers, before the legislation became effective. Publication of this letter in the *Teacher Advocate* emphasized the need for this protective legislation.[24] ISTA continued to press for improved due process legislation throughout the remainder of the twentieth century. As a result, due process was expanded in 1989 and again in 1991, the latter law requiring due process before suspending teachers without pay.[25]

Although PL 217 did not offer "right to strike" protection, teachers continued to use strikes as the way to win pay increases and to change working conditions in the 1970s. For example, the Marion Teachers Association (MTA) had been negotiating for eighteen months, with no agreement in sight, when 388 of the 517 teachers in the school corporation walked out on August 29, 1978. Although many tried to avert the strike, an agreement could not be reached on six issues: grievance procedures, the length of the teacher day, class size, the number of teaching periods, salary, and health and life insurance. The school board immediately asked for, and received, restraining orders against the leaders of the local association. On August 30, seven men and one woman, members of the teachers' negotiating team, were jailed for their part in the strike. The "Marion 8" joined the ranks of a growing number of militant local leaders who were willing to go to jail for their union. After a long list of proposals and counterproposals from both sides, including a compromise proposal drafted by an IEERB-appointed mediator, the strike ended "with little emotion" on September 7, 1978.[26]

In August of the same year, a dispute arose in east-central Indiana between members of the Richmond Association of Classroom Teachers (RACT) and the Richmond School Board. Seventy-two percent of Richmond's teaching staff walked out when RACT refused to accept the school board's offer of an 8.5 percent pay raise. IEERB appointed a negotiator to mediate, and by August 29, 1978, RACT agreed to enter binding arbitration. The school board, however, was not as willing to settle. Publicly a member of the school board blamed the impasse on the striking teachers: "your indication that the RACT decided to resolve the crisis is surprising. The only crisis . . . is the illegal strike called by the RACT."[27] Standing firm, the school board approved a budget that did not include wage increases demanded by teachers. The board claimed that money was not available, but a former county auditor told the board, "If you have to raise taxes to reopen our schools the community of Richmond will support you." Community support was running nearly three to one in support of the teachers. Finally, the teachers and the board came to a tentative agreement, and the strike ended. The new pay raise would cost the school corporation $125,000, and the teachers gave up three demands relating to class size, teacher preparation time, and due process.[28]

By the 1980s, strikes were occurring less often. A typical bargaining session brought administrators, school board members, and representatives from the school board's law firm to the table opposite a bargaining team from the local teachers' association. The bargaining team for the teachers usually was comprised of their elected representatives, but sometimes the director of the UniServ district served on it as well.[29] While the sessions were often contentious, the two sides were usually willing to negotiate a contract. As a result, teachers were gaining more control in their workplace.

Ronald Jensen's tenure brought many positive changes for teachers in ISTA. Under his watch, teacher unity became a byword. Unification had made UniServ possible, which provided assistance to local associations in the areas of collective bargaining and teachers' rights. Contracts were negotiated in a more objective manner, and power was realigned away from established bureaucracies toward the members of the teaching profession. As the conflicts in Marion and Richmond demonstrate, the passage of PL 217 did not end the adversarial relationships between the teachers' union and local school boards. However, in most situations, contracts were resolved without strikes once teachers made known their willingness to strike. Once organized, teachers were now members of a labor union.

The Local Bargaining Association

A veteran teacher in the Mount Vernon school system and a leader in ISTA during the 1980s, John Ransford was also involved in bargaining as a representative of the local association. In 2000 he described his experiences: *I'll talk a little bit about the process of the local and I am speaking of mine. We would always go to the teacher[s] with a survey: "What are some of the concerns that are really affecting you? What are some of the things you are thinking?" Then after gathering these, we would develop a set of goals on our own. (I hoped that the opposing side of the table did not know what our goals were.) And we would propose a contract, an item-by-item issue in the contract. Of course, the opposing superintendent would counter-propose with a contract. And it was just a back-and-forth kind of thing. You knew you had some things in your proposal that you could give up, but maybe one or two teachers were concerned about. Some issues that a majority of teachers wanted were the last thing we would ever give up. And of course, salaries were big, but another thing was the fringe benefits.*

In Mount Vernon we were always real concerned with class size, and we were one of the locals that maintained a very low teacher-pupil ratio. . . . Before the law [Project Prime Time] passed, in the elementary system we had about a 20 to 1 ratio . . . that's what we had. We had that all the time. Now in some other schools in the area we had 35-some plus students . . . the biggest class I ever had was 24 in all of my classes. I think our teachers realized that yes, we are going to work for less, but we are going to have a better teacher-pupil ratio. So I think our teachers were smart in that way and I should give credit to the superintendent. Leave time . . . we were one of the leaders in our area to increase the personal leave days, to increase the number of sick days, things like that.

Then a couple of times we even got hung up on an issue with the superintendent's bargaining team, which by the way had hired an outsider to do their bargaining for them. (And we called him "the hired gun.") But anyway sometimes the hired guns were easier to bargain with than the administrators because they knew how to bargain. One of the big difficulties was . . . a lot of the administrators hadn't learned the art of bargaining. Through ISTA and the training sessions, some of the local leaders or bargainers got to be quite artful. In fact, the present president [of ISTA] Dave Young [J. David Young] was one of the first to bargain and he was one of the first that went out on strike and he was actually jailed. I think one of the things the superintendents worried about was school shutting down because of strikes, but there weren't that many strikes in Indiana . . . and I really don't think the teachers really wanted to strike but they wanted that right if they ever needed it.

ISTA demonstrated its commitment to minority participation in the teaching profession with its Affirmative Action Plan. ISTA Archives.

Staff member Robert Barcus consults with others from the Indiana delegation at the 1974 NEA Convention. ISTA Archives.

Cordell Affeldt was thrust into the presidency of ISTA with the death of Ray Gran on February 13, 1978. Affeldt served tirelessly from 1978 to 1982, keeping ISTA's larger mission before a state, local, and national audience. NEA Communications Services.

In 1979, NEA board member Joanna Hock gives the victory salute after teachers successfully lobbied for the passage of the Department of Education bill. President Carter later signed the bill into law. NEA Communications Services.

Warren Williams donned a hard hat before he made his daily rounds, checking the construction progress on the ISTA headquarters. ISTA Archives.

ISTA dedicated its renovated building with a black tie gala; Warren Williams stands at the microphone, and Damon Moore mans the light switch. ISTA Archives.

The statehouse reflected in the new glass exterior of the ISTA Center. The reflection symbolized the impact that political decision had on the business of education and vice versa. ISTA Archives.

Cartoonists both lampooned ISTA and paid testimony to its influence in the legislature with their humor. ISTA Archives.

The "Presidents Plus Two" day, established in 1980, represented an opportunity for the local presidents and two other teachers from each association to join colleagues for a day at the statehouse. This visit included time with the governor. ISTA Archives.

X

A Powerhouse in the Statehouse

During the last quarter of the twentieth century, ISTA was a true "powerhouse in the statehouse."[1] With the establishment of I-PACE (a political action committee) in 1973 and with the increased personal commitment of individual teachers to take a more active political role at the local and state level, ISTA's influence in the political spectrum became more directed and, therefore, more effective. At issue were the age-old questions: How would Indiana's public school system be funded and reformed? Who would set the qualification standards for the teaching profession? ISTA remained constant in its advocacy for increased funding for schools, but now individual members of the Association took ISTA's case to the statehouse in an attempt to secure control of their profession and to protect the rights of teachers. As Cordell Affeldt, then president of ISTA, said, "We embraced bargaining. We embraced political action. In our maturity we close[d] the circle by embracing a new professionalism. Miss Brooks and Mr. Peepers [two affable teachers in situation comedies of the 1950s] have grown up."[2]

The political orientation of Miss Brooks and Mr. Peepers had changed, indeed, as the torch was passed from one generation to the next. In fact, 1973 has often been called a crucial year, for this was the year that education became intensely politicized with the passage of Public Law 217.

ICTA, once the Indiana State Federation of Public School Teachers, merged with ISTA, thereby creating the most effective bargaining coalition for teachers in Indiana.

About this same time, superintendents, principals, and administrators left ISTA. According to some, Robert Wyatt wrote a letter to "management" informing them that their membership as supervisors was inconsistent with the future mission and organization of ISTA as a union. (No documentary evidence of this letter has been found.) From a practical standpoint, the passage of PL 217 placed teachers and the superintendents and administrators on opposite sides of the bargaining table as the participants in a labor-management scenario. Some superintendents may have felt pressure from their contemporaries to leave ISTA after its unionization— commonly argued among contemporaries as "How could you support an organization that doesn't want you anymore?" Whatever the reason, superintendents, principals, and administrators left the ranks of ISTA in the first years of unification of the local, state, and national teachers associations.[3]

In addition to the passage of PL 217, 1973 dealt another blow to school superintendents. Governor Otis Bowen won the election, in part, on his promise of tax reductions; he achieved part of this promised reduction by freezing all property tax levies at the 1973 level while allowing assessed valuations to increase. In other words, the immediate impact on superintendents was less money to meet their individual corporation needs, particularly in salaries and other personnel-related costs. Hence, Indiana's school superintendents in 1973 experienced two major changes in the workplace; they now had to engage in collective bargaining with their teachers, and they had to accomplish this feat with no additional funds to negotiate teacher salary demands.[4]

Another groundbreaking move occurred in 1973 when ISTA formed I-PACE, Indiana Political Action Committee for Education, a legal entity that provided monetary support for political candidates endorsed by the Association. Initially, teachers were asked to donate ten dollars a year to I-PACE, which was set up as a corporation separate from ISTA.[5] (Later the amount was raised to twelve and then twenty-four dollars a year.)[6] ISTA was already the largest lobby for education in the state, but the presence of local political action committees (PACs) gave ISTA additional clout in the political arena.[7] Establishing a network of local PACs was not an easy task but one that Robert Margraf, chief lobbyist for ISTA, readily accepted. He organized PACs in Lake County and Evansville, but encountered difficulty in other areas of the state. He was fond of saying that he had PACs from one end of the state to the other; however, at least initially, he had none between the two extremes.[8] When UniServ districts were instituted around the state, executive director Ronald Jensen and Margraf decided to establish a PAC in each district, with the local UniServ director as the treasurer.[9]

While ISTA had long endorsed candidates "friendly" to education, I-PACE now allowed the organization a legal means to donate money for political campaigns. No money from the state association went to national elections, so members were encouraged to contribute separately to NEA-PAC, which supported candidates at the national level. Clearly, one political party was more "friendly" to education than the other and benefited more from these contributions; at the first I-PACE/NEAPAC workshop, the NEA gave all Democrats "A" grades and failed all Republicans on a test focused on voting issues.[10] Notably, that same year was a resounding success for candidates supported by I-PACE with eighty-three of the ninety-eight endorsed candidates (or 84.6 percent) winning their races.[11] Indeed, political action became key to the strategic and tactical goals of ISTA, for, as Margraf astutely pointed out, "all decisions affecting teachers and education are political."[12] The endorsement of the PACs could make or break a candidacy.

What made Margraf an effective lobbyist for ISTA in the statehouse was not *his* power, but the power of the teachers that he could muster at a moment's notice to stage a rally or to initiate a letter-writing campaign. By the 1980s, ISTA's legislative department was coordinating a visitation day to give the rank and file the opportunity to visit the Indiana General Assembly each Thursday that it was in session.[13] During Cordell Affeldt's tenure as president, an annual legislative visitation day called "Presidents Plus Two" was instituted. On this day the president and two teachers from each local visited the statehouse, attended meetings, and lunched with their representatives and senators.[14] This increased activity was especially important as ISTA battled the funding cuts of the 1980s.

These were difficult times for educators. There was a growing disillusionment with the huge cost of liberal programs that sprang from Lyndon Johnson's Great Society, and conservatives were moving to reduce government spending. In 1981, the first year of Ronald Reagan's presidency,

ISTA actively lobbied to protest a proposed 25 percent reduction in federal funding for education. Although eleven teachers and two staff members left for Washington, D.C., to participate in NEA's Congressional Contact Team program and Affeldt testified before a Congressional Committee as to the disastrous effects of reduced federal funding on Indiana and its teachers, this was the year that Congress passed the first of the federal budget cuts in education.[15]

Educators and education were under fire once more. As Indiana's manufacturing base shrank, jobs were lost. To counteract this, state government was seeking businesses to relocate to the state, and education was key to enticing these businesses. However, Indiana's educational system did not rank near the top nationally. The number of children being "home schooled" rose.[16] Conservatives, who were dubbed the "New Right," called for a new agenda for reform: standardized testing; state aid to private schools, including tuition tax credits and vouchers; censorship of textbooks; and residency requirements for teachers were features of their program.

At this time ISTA and then-governor Robert Orr began an often times adversarial relationship. In 1981, acting executive director Dale Harris expressed concern over the "drastic cuts" in education and despaired that "the future of Indiana's children is in jeopardy."[17] Cleverly, that year ISTA participants at the rallies sent "oars" to Governor Orr pleading that "he lift his political anchor, use his oar and move the Ship of State ahead."[18] ISTA and its membership intensified efforts to influence legislative decisions. For example, in the fall of 1983 eighty teachers attended the fourth annual ISTA Political Action Workshop, where they studied not only how to lobby, but also some of the issues that would define the rest of the decade: merit pay, tuition tax credits, and retirement cutbacks.[19] However, it was apparent that only a small cadre of educators supported ISTA's lobbying efforts with time and money; a mere 1.5 percent of the membership contributed 42.2 percent of I-PACE's budget.[20]

During this time, Affeldt continued to reinforce the importance of political action. "Influencing the State House decisions remains the most basic service that ISTA can offer teachers across the state."[21] Hence, in 1984 at the Representative Assembly, 700 delegates debated making contributions to I-PACE through an "options guaranteed" program, a payroll deduction that was earmarked for I-PACE. It was called "options guaranteed" because the deduction was made automatically, unless teachers requested not to have it made or opted out of the plan. (Up to this point, donations had been purely voluntary.) Over some vigorous objections, "options guaranteed" passed by a two-to-one margin; the financial underpinning for I-PACE was assured.[22]

Such changes in political action were deemed necessary, in part, to mount an effective answer to "Phase II of the Decade of Excellence," Governor Orr's sweeping educational reform. Introduced just after "A Nation at Risk," a national report on education, had called for widespread reform of the educational system, "Phase II of the Decade of Excellence" included initiatives for improving the quality of education, such as Project Prime Time, merit pay, and right-to-work bills.[23] Project Prime Time provided a monetary reimbursement to school corporations that reduced teacher-student ratios in kindergarten through third grade.[24] This was a universally applauded objective and a program supported by ISTA. At the same time, Orr's administration had restructured the State Board of Education. The board's three commissions (teacher training and licensing, textbooks, and general education), which had been instituted by Wyatt in 1943, were replaced with a single eleven-member board.[25] Teachers wondered what this change would mean for them.

Three years later, another of Orr's initiatives, the A+ Program for Educational Excellence, was passed as PL 390-1987. This legislation incorporated approximately thirteen separate initiatives that ran the gamut from Performance-Based Accreditation to a Beginning Teacher Internship Program to a Committee on Educational Attitudes, Motivation, and Parental Involvement. The A+ Program also contained controversial elements, such as a longer school year and mandated testing. ISTEP (Indiana State Testing of Educational Progress) tests became a key element in evaluating the performance of schools and teachers. ISTA had long endorsed higher standards for high-school graduation, but it did not endorse ISTEP testing.[26] Executive director Warren Williams had warned that ISTEP testing would "systematically brand 16 percent of Indiana's school kids as failures."[27] An ISTA in-house survey of ISTEP revealed "high anxiety levels" on the part of teachers, parents, and students at testing time. Twenty-five percent of teachers reported they had been advised to change their teaching to "fit the test."[28]

Conservatives thought education would improve only if teachers and principals were held accountable for poor student performance, while ISTA continued to support the long-held belief that increased funding was the key to improving public education. ISTA's position was bolstered by a study funded by the Lilly Endowment and released in 1985, which found that "Indiana already has an efficient education system. The problem is . . . the state does not commit enough resources to create the quality system its political leaders say they want or the state's economic future needs."[29] Spurred by the lobbying efforts of ISTA, the state increased funding for education. Within a ten-year span from 1982 to 1992, expenditures per student grew nearly 21 percent.[30] However, it was merit pay and accountability that became the focus of the public's attention.

Superficially, merit pay seemed like an "all-American issue" that rewarded good teachers, but it was infinitely more complex than that. First of all, merit pay was inconsistent with the philosophy of unionism. Teachers who remembered being held hostage to the whims of township trustees, superintendents, and school boards at contract renewal time cringed at the thought of subjective evaluations being part of the negotiating process once more. If teacher merit pay was correlated to student performance, how could or would adjustments be made for environmental and capacity factors—"pre-existing conditions," as they were called? Who would evaluate—students, other teachers, or professional administrators? Would teachers control the profession? Who would set the standards?[31] As Damon Moore, president of ISTA in 1984, had warned educators: "Evaluations [of teachers] in this state have for too long been based on a mixture of sentimentality, administrative self-interest, and voodoo smoke."[32]

ISTA called for monetary incentives to attract the best and brightest to the profession of teaching. However, the state was considering lowering teaching standards in order to broaden the pool of available teachers.[33] Although the state was facing a teacher shortage at a time when Project Prime Time was reducing class size and creating a need for more teachers, Moore and others at ISTA called for raising teaching standards: "if we're not careful, the state bureaucracy that is busy handing out 'emergency certificates' and lowering standards could be placed in charge of a state board for establishing professional teaching standards."[34]

The climate of political reform changed immediately after the 1988 gubernatorial election. ISTA helped elect Evan Bayh as governor over John Mutz, who had been Orr's lieutenant governor. Evan Bayh was the son of former U.S. senator Birch Bayh, a longtime advocate of public education and the NEA since his service in the Indiana General Assembly. With Evan Bayh as governor, ISTA was able to secure passage of much legislation in the Indiana General Assembly.

In the next eight years ISTA realized many gains for teachers' rights if not for educational reform. In 1989 alone, ISTA was able to secure passage of an early retirement law and home rule legislation for school corporations. Funds from the state lottery were dedicated to reducing the unfunded liability of the Teachers Retirement Fund (a volatile issue since Wyatt had first discovered that governors were withholding funds to balance the state budget). In addition, due process for teachers was expanded and newspapers were no longer allowed to publish the individual salaries of teachers. In the next long session of the General Assembly in 1991, funding was passed for computer technology, special education for preschool, latchkey services for preschool children, and Medicaid reimbursement to schools for services to eligible children.[35] In addition, ISTA was able to secure passage of its long-desired Professional Standards Board, which allowed teachers to set the standards for teacher training and licensing, realizing the end of a more than hundred-year quest.[36] Bayh was so "friendly" to education that during his last session as governor, he told teachers that they were "doing the Lord's work as they prepared to lobby the General Assembly."[37]

The 1990s were, however, trying years for ISTA at the statehouse, even though both Bayh and his successor, Frank O'Bannon, were considered "friendly" to education. ISTA continued to be a force in education, so much so that the *Indianapolis Star* labeled it a "political behemoth," both "feared and respected for its power and influence." However, even after expending $311,000 to influence state races in 1994, ISTA saw "fair share" (dues paid by non-members to defray expenses incurred by union representatives) stricken from the books by the General Assembly the following year. Executive Director Warren Williams charged, "Republicans vengefully killed fair share to wound ISTA." Overriding the veto of Governor Evan Bayh, Republican lawmakers made it illegal for the Association to collect fair share payments from non-members or for local teacher's contracts to include fair share provisions.[38]

Fair share had been difficult for ISTA to enforce, in any case. Since the court-approved imposition of fair share in 1982, ISTA and local affiliates had repeatedly sued non-payers to force compliance. Teachers who were philosophically in opposition to some of the stances taken by NEA fought the enforced payment of fair share fees, even though the money supported collective bargaining activities and not, as some fair share opponents asserted, the more controversial programs supported by NEA.[39]

In 1995, ISTA suffered another setback in the legislature. That year, the General Assembly singled out the Indianapolis Education Association (IEA) for a rollback of past contract negotiation gains by passing a law that severely limited the ability of IEA to negotiate with the Indianapolis public school corporation. IEA charged that this law was unconstitutional and filed suit. In December 1995, a Marion County Superior Court judge ruled against the IEA. The newly passed law, which was neatly hidden within the text of a larger bill, stated that the union (IEA) could negotiate only on issues linked to wages (salaries and money-related fringe benefits) but could no longer negotiate over such items as rules governing teacher transfers, working conditions, and grievances.[40] For each gain in the legislature, it seemed, ISTA suffered a setback.

Conservatives had made inroads during the last two decades of the twentieth century with their vision of educational reform. Leaders of ISTA felt that reform based on accountability was fundamentally flawed and not supportive of public education. Reform could not occur without considering the social conditions that impair education: poverty and the home environment of the students. In other words, teachers in schools with higher percentages of at-risk children should not be held to the same accountability standards as teachers in affluent suburban schools. Similarly, ISTA feared that the move of tax money to private education through vouchers and tax credits would create a two-tier educational system: the "haves," who could afford elite private school; and the "have-nots," who were served by the public school system.[41] ISTA's reform agenda included increased salaries and benefits, smaller classes, teacher-controlled standards, and teacher training.

ISTA continued to fight against growing demands by legislators and taxpayers for educational reforms based on bottom-line, test-score accountability and to support its own reform program. In the 2000 presidential election, both George W. Bush and Al Gore ran on platforms that emphasized reform in education testimony to the level of public concern over educational issues. Then the following year, the U.S. Congress passed an education bill that required tests in reading and math every year in grades three through eight and once students were in high school, provided money for charter schools and allowed students in failing schools to use federal funds for transportation to other public schools or for tutoring.[42] That same year, the Indiana General Assembly passed a law that mandated testing beyond that required at the federal level and provided financial incentives for schools where students performed well on tests. In a turnabout from its earlier position against ISTEP, ISTA's president gave lukewarm support for this testing, calling this "a remarkable program" but expressing concern for those schools that did not "make the mark."[43]

In the last years of the century, it was clear that conservative forces had set themselves in opposition to ISTA, but the Association had made gains in generating funds for public education and in gaining rights for teachers. As proof of ISTA's ability to lobby, expenditures per child increased dramatically as Indiana moved from a national rank of thirty-second in 1972 to fourteenth by 2001.[44] Indiana was putting more funds into public education than ever before, and teachers had made legal gains in their rights. The establishment of I-PACE had allowed ISTA to summon support from across the state to elect legislators and to influence votes on issues important to teachers and education. No longer did ISTA rely on the force of one man's personality or his personal relationships with legislators. By 1988, nearly 75 percent of Hoosier teachers reported an inclination to vote for candidates endorsed by I-PACE, even when they considered themselves "independent" of any party affiliation, a degree of support few other organizations could match.[45] That same year the *Indianapolis Star* reported that "the mere mention of the Indiana State Teachers Association can do two things to a state legislator: prompt a surly scowl or elicit an enthusiastic endorsement."[46] Legislators listened to ISTA; its base of support through teacher lobbyists made it "a powerhouse in the statehouse." The simple characters of television history, Miss Brooks and Mr. Peepers, had, indeed, grown up—and grown strong.

School Desegregation

In the midst of vast transformations occurring in ISTA in the early 1970s, Indianapolis was confronted with the charge of "creating desegregated, nonracially identifiable schools." Few issues in education were as politically charged as desegregation, for it touched the core of people's attitudes about race and culture. In 1949, Indiana had begun the process to desegregate schools gradually, but that effort had stalled until the 1960s and the early 1970s, when the focus on civil rights brought renewed attention to the inherent inequalities of racially segregated schools. In 1968, a complaint led the Federal Department of Justice to file suit against the Indianapolis Public Schools for violation of the Civil Rights Act of 1964. IPS responded that residential patterns defined its school population. In reality, residential segregation, a remnant from the years before fair housing laws, indeed created racially separate schools. Nonetheless Judge S. Hugh Dillin found that IPS had practiced de jure segregation and ordered its schools desegregated.[47]

The desegregation order affected not only IPS, but also twenty-two other Indiana school corporations. With its current emphasis on teachers' rights, ISTA members resolved "to hereby unite . . . to accomplish what is necessary and possible to protect the rights of teachers in the affected corporations . . . and to work with school corporations to insure that the educational environment is conducive to maximizing the potential for learning for all students."[48] Then ISTA filed a petition to enter the suit in order to protect the rights of teachers. In doing so, ISTA was not "taking a pro-busing or anti-busing stance," according to executive director Ronald Jensen, who stated that the organization was only "interested in the jobs of teachers and in the quality of education."[49] That fall, when it was clear that desegregation for all cities was inevitable, the Fort Wayne school system, which was facing forced compliance, and the Fort Wayne Education Association began to work together to help desegregate schools in "a smooth and rational fashion."[50]

In 1979, Judge Dillin issued a decision that Marion County schools would have to begin busing 8,711 black children to suburban schools in the 1979–1980 school year. This was not a popular decision with parent groups. ISTA was not concerned with the merit of the order but with the protection of student and teacher rights and jobs. In fact, desegregation did cost jobs. For those teachers who retained their positions, ISTA advocated training to help them deal with the problems that inevitably arose in schools with a new racial mix.[51] ISTA's approach to the realities of desegregation illustrated the present orientation of the Association: to protect the jobs of teachers and to maintain a safe teaching environment.

XI

Rebuilding Years

In the last two decades of the twentieth century the Indiana State Teachers Association marshaled its efforts to rebuild and refocus after the chaotic years of the 1970s. Grassroots political activism had allowed ISTA's lobbying arm to become its most visible branch. Strikes and success at the bargaining table had enabled its union arm to become its most powerful. However, members of ISTA saw themselves as professionals. This multidimensional character created a need to recast ISTA's organizational image if the quest for professional development was not to be lost within the rhetoric of unionism. In these years, ISTA remodeled its headquarters and invested in technology. At times, it concentrated on refocusing on the needs of children through various conferences and think tanks as its members sought new ways to fulfill its original charge to advance the cause of public education. Yet the struggle to control the profession of teaching in the legislature, the fight for the rights of teachers in the local associations, and the battle for fiscal solvency consumed much of its organizational energy.

Internal change had come painfully. Executive director Ronald Jensen left in December 1979, and Dale Harris, after serving as acting director for a few months, was hired to replace him. Change in leadership did not end the internal struggles for authority. In 1982, as ISTA continued to grapple with organizational realignment, Harris spoke of the "fragile understanding" of members concerning the roles of governance groups, the staff, and the "executive director as the manager of staff and day-to-day operation." Clearly Harris felt that the roles had been "improperly mixed" during the era of staff reductions in the late 1970s, and he was committed to bringing them back into balance.[1] Within three years, however, Harris resigned and Vincent M. Kiernan took over as acting director.

In 1985, the board, recognizing the need for a fresh approach, hired Warren Williams. Williams, like Jensen, was a seasoned veteran from the "Michigan Mafia" and a nationally known activist who had traveled to teachers associations around the United States, advising them on how to negotiate and strike. As a UniServ director in Michigan, Williams was known as a "strategist."[2] A strategist was needed to help ISTA mount its challenge against the educational reform agenda of Governor Robert Orr.

Damon Moore, as president of ISTA, had already charted a new course before Williams's arrival. Appropriately, the membership of ISTA, the majority of whom had been weaned on the rhetoric of the civil rights movement of the 1960s and 1970s, had elected Moore, an African American, as president of the Association in 1983. Dramatic and flamboyant, sometimes to a fault, Moore addressed both the old issues, such as teachers' rights, and new ones, such as programming for at-risk children and instructing teachers on how to avoid charges of immorality or misconduct.[3] He reinforced the idea that teachers did important work: "we are in the middle of the time in our history unmatched in the enormity of both danger and opportunity for public schools and the teachers in them." He challenged teachers to meet the "danger and opportunity."[4]

Together Moore and Williams brought ISTA into the technology age. They installed computers in the headquarters and began to talk about electronic mail as early as 1985.[5] They revamped Center Print, an in-house printing operation that was foundering in 1985, and installed updated equipment and invested in new technology rather than send work to other print shops. An In-Service Corporation was set up to provide in-service training and professional development to members through conferences and software. (This corporation became inactive in the 1990s.) A Video Conferencing Center never fully developed, but it represented the goal of leadership to be on the cutting edge of technology.[6] These initiatives, however, were expensive for the Association.

One of the most expensive changes of this period was the remodeling of the ISTA Center. As part of Williams's keynote address in 1986, he spoke of the problems that he saw developing with the building. It was not producing income and had become a liability; tenants were leaving because it was outdated and rundown. Concurrently, Williams was approached by a group of investors who wished to purchase the ISTA Center. The board decided not to sell the building and instead opted to renovate it. Williams realized that ISTA was in an enviable position of being on the leading edge of office building development in Indianapolis; but other ventures in office construction were in the offing. If the renovation were to be done, it needed to be done quickly. Williams warned the board that this was going to be difficult; some people would not like it, but he said, "You don't ever win unless you raise the risk level."[7]

The board decided to "raise the risk level" for this rebuilding project. Ground was broken, and work began on an addition just north of the ISTA Center on land already owned by the Association. Tenants were moved to other areas of the building as renovation proceeded floor by floor. As the renovation process moved forward, the full extent of the problem of asbestos contamination was revealed. ISTA had been aware that the building contained asbestos, but the final cost of its removal was more than four times the original estimate. With mounting costs came the inevitable controversy; too much money was being spent. Members remembered the recent past when ISTA had pulled itself from a financial abyss. Divisive rumors circulated that the elevators in the renovated building were to be paneled in gold and that the president and the executive director were to have faucets made of gold in their private bathrooms. (The new offices of the executive director and the president *were* spacious, with balconies symbolically overlooking the Capitol, and, as a gift from the builder, their initials were engraved on their bathroom faucets—but the fixtures were not golden.)[8]

The major problem with the remodeling project occurred when ISTA tried to secure its final financing and mortgage. Merchants National Bank, the construction loan lender, decided not to write the mortgage—neither would the other two larger Indianapolis banks, American Fletcher National Bank and INB National Bank. That year, it seemed to Williams and the board that the politics of educational reform were coming back to haunt ISTA as it was being squeezed by the business community. This was an election year, and Evan Bayh, who was endorsed by ISTA, was running against John Mutz, a man of influence with the business community. Williams remembered being "in meetings in the executive committee room where you just felt the tension from the standpoint of the bankers feeling that they could hold on and put us out of business, [so] that we would not be fighting them in the political election." ISTA eventually went to the First of America Bank in Speedway for financing and found other state teachers associations that were willing to assist. In addition, NEA allowed the Association to defer some dues to help ease the cash flow; this loan was then converted to an interest-bearing note.[9]

Issues concerning the building renovation continued to divide the membership. Some felt that the remodeling and the opening party were extravagant. Instead of the expensive opening gala that was held, with a steak dinner and music furnished by a nationally known band, some members thought a spaghetti dinner would have been more in order.[10] Then membership was asked to increase its dues five dollars a year per member for five years to pay off the construction loan. It did so, but the building and its accompanying financial woes remained a contentious issue. It was certainly an issue in the next ISTA presidential election, when Garrett Harbron ran on a platform of fiscal conservatism against Damon Moore. At issue, too, was the fact that Moore had already served a two-year term and a three-year term; his supporters contended he was eligible for another term because he had not served the six years allowed in the revised bylaws. His detractors thought otherwise. Harbron, who had been treasurer while Cordell Affeldt was president, won the election by only a few votes.[11]

The election of Harbron over Moore and the events of the late 1980s had a lingering impact on the organization. In the 1990s, people spoke of "camps" or "factions" within the organization, one conservative and one liberal. Politically, the differences appeared to be minimal; one member saw it as a matter of style rather than substance. The Moore faction disputed that notion and believed that with the passing of his think tanks and other innovative ideas about education, fiscal solvency had become more important than children and their education. The other camp felt that fiscal responsibility was necessary for ISTA to continue to advance the cause of both teachers and education.[12]

Financial stability and financial services for members were important objectives for the long-term viability of the Association. In 1986, ISTA established a separate corporation, the ISTA Insurance Trust, headed by Bruce Rogers. The trust was set up to provide a range of insurance options for its members that included life, health, dental, vision, and pharmaceutical insurance, at competitive rates. These plans were tailored to meet the needs of negotiating teams and were oriented to benefit individual teachers.[13] It took several years for the trust to get off the ground, but by the 1990s, it was profitable. In 1993, ISTA established its Financial Services Corporation (FSC) as a wholly owned subsidiary of ISTA. Former president of ISTA Garrett Harbron was chosen in 1996 to direct the FSC, which was set up to provide to individuals a range of financial services—namely 403b Retirement Savings Plans, Section 125 Flexible Benefits Programs, Medicare Supplement Insurance Program, Long Term Care Insurance, and financial workshops—which were not part of the Insurance Trust.[14] Then in 1997, the Administrative Services Corporation, a wholly owned for-profit subsidiary of ISTA, was established to handle the claims arising from the trust.[15]

Teachers' rights, including minority employment rights, were an ongoing concern. As a result, ISTA, in continuing and strengthening an organizational policy that dated from 1974, developed its affirmative action plan in 1981. Revised again in 1999, it targeted employment of "minorities and women in percentages at least equal to their representation in the population from which the Association seeks job applicants," but not at the expense of the "status of current employees." The goal was to increase employment percentages to reflect the population of the Indianapolis Standard Metropolitan Statistical Area (SMSA) and to direct recruitment to accomplish this. The executive director reported on the organizational progress of this plan to the board of directors each summer at the Leadership Conference.[16]

As the twentieth century gave way to the twenty-first, ISTA began to refocus its goals and objectives. It organized six strategic teams—Membership, Member Rights, Legislative, Political Action, School Quality, and Public Relations—to develop a plan to implement governance more fully.[17] As part of its emphasis on professional development, ISTA cosponsored

Goals 2000: Educate America Act. In doing so, it offered support for partnerships among school corporations, local affiliates, and higher-education institutions.[18] The thrust of Goals 2000 was to re-involve educators at all levels in discussions and decisions on the philosophy and direction of public education and the teaching profession. Associations and corporations with a direct relationship to public-school teachers were considered associated entities of ISTA. They included Indiana Retired Teachers Association (IRTA), Indiana Student Education Association (ISEA), ISTA Insurance Trust, Indiana Political Action Committee for Education, ISTA In-Service Corporation, ISTA Financial Services, and local education associations.[19]

J. David Young, ISTA's soft-spoken president from 1995 to 2001, said of ISTA's focus: "defining and measuring quality—for students, for teachers and for schools—are central. . . . We should take responsibility because we will consider both results and opportunities and because we can organize schools which enable students to succeed, not fail."[20] Young believed that collective bargaining remained key to "improving teacher quality, school capacity, and student learning."[21] He acknowledged that the Association had sometimes lost its way and that it needed to refocus on professional issues. Yet, as outgoing president Young worried that the next generation would not understand the value of collective bargaining for teachers and for the development of the profession.[22]

Appropriately, Young's successor, Judith Briganti, brought a change in focus to the Association as it celebrated its 150th anniversary. As vice president, Briganti had been involved in licensing and re-certification issues as a member of the Professional Standards Board. Part of her advocacy as president was to give teachers the tools that they needed to succeed, whether it was in contract negotiations or teacher training. Unlike her predecessors, Briganti saw the move toward accountability as an asset that allowed teachers to measure both their own success and their students' achievement in the classroom. Like her predecessors, Briganti recognized the difficulty of such accountability standards for teachers of inner-city children, for she herself had taught in an inner-city school in northern Indiana.[23] Briganti brought a unique advocacy for teachers and children in advancing the cause of education.

The new president did not have much transition time to focus on this new advocacy in the early months of her tenure. Briganti and the Association faced a recurring challenge to education in 2002 as Indiana's much-lauded budget surplus evaporated in the face of reduced tax revenues and a general downturn in the nation's economy. As part of his extensive budget cuts to decrease the future deficit, Governor Frank O'Bannon proposed paring the education budget by nearly $450 million, which would affect education in Indiana at all levels. There were even rumors that the state's contributions to the Teacher's Retirement Fund might be affected by the governor's actions; similar manipulations of these same funds had caused the Association, during Robert Wyatt's years, to sue the state on at least two previous occasions. The immediate fallout of the final budget cuts was felt in schools in the 2002 fall term. Some teachers lost their jobs; plans for advances in educational technology were shelved; part-time instructional aide positions were eliminated; and some top-level staff took early retirement to ease the financial burden on some school corporations.[24] It was a scenario all too familiar to senior members of ISTA.

As the twenty-first century began, one generation of leaders of ISTA was relinquishing control of the organization and passing its collective knowledge to the next. The Association was in a transitional stage, an era of continued rebuilding. For some members, it was hard to get beyond the struggles to gain collective bargaining and to advance teachers' rights; they felt ISTA was first and foremost a union. For others, there was a sense of loss with the passing of the excitement they found in the think tanks and symposia of the 1980s; for them ISTA should be, first and foremost, a professional organization. When Cordell Affeldt said in 1983, "We embraced bargaining. We embraced political action. In our maturity we close the circle by embracing the new professionalism," she was perhaps uttering a hope more than a reality for teachers in the 1980s and 1990s. This teaching generation had been defined by unionism, grassroots advocacy, and participatory democracy, but not by great advances in professional issues. As Briganti raised issues of a new advocacy, teachers wondered: What would define the next generation? Who would guide it? How would the cause of education be advanced?

The In-Service Corporation

Damon Moore, president of ISTA from 1983 to 1988, reflected in 2000: *We established a 501c3 not-for-profit corporation called the ISTA In-Service Corporation. The purpose of the In-Service Corporation was to deal with some of these emerging issues of professionalism, to deal with certification standards, to deal with what teachers needed professionally. The In-Service Corporation was put together, and it had a board that included laypeople, local superintendents, as well as our leadership. We got one grant from, I think it was the state department of education, to deal with a couple of issues, one of them being teacher professionalism. What does that mean?*

We'd have what we call think tanks . . . and we'd bring people together, lock them up all weekend. We'd pay for them to come. We would pay superintendents or school boards at half-day of sub pay so that we could get those people in there. We'd bring them in Friday; we treated them royally; we fed them well; we worked them to death. They never left the premises. . . . We'd take like two floors. They could go sleep when they wanted to but there was a think-tank situation where we kept them together until they got things done. And we have four or five documents . . . from those [sessions]—we called them Presidential Symposia. We talked about issues well ahead of their time. We talked about professional issues before most people in the nation were ready to deal with it. We were ahead. One of my bad things is getting ahead of my time. Timing is everything. And if you miss it, you miss it . . .

We had a task force that studied home schooling and the impact on public schools in the '80s. Nobody wanted to talk about it. We had a joint group that worked on discipline procedures, working with the superintendents' and the principals' associations. . . . But those issues changed ISTA's image. . . . I'll proudly say, during my tenure in office, there was not an educational meeting in this state, unless we were there and by us being there, I mean a representative number of teachers. I can't say that anymore. I've been to major decision-making meetings as a member of a commission and no ISTA representation [was present]. They wouldn't dare have thought of having a meeting about education without ISTA during that time, when I was here.

Professional Standards

In 2001 Judith Briganti, president of ISTA, reflected on her tenure when she was vice president of the Association and served on the Professional Standards Board. *I wasn't there when the Professional Standards Board was formed. I was on the periphery. I knew about things that were happening in regards to that. But the whole point of it was—at least looking from the outside in and then having served on the board—was wanting the teaching profession to take charge and to make sure there were quality individuals in the classroom for every child in the state. And who better to help make those decisions of who should be licensed and who should not be, than teachers? And as the board was expanded there was a teacher majority at first, but then it was expanded to have others. I know it was a passion of Damon Moore's, and a vision for many people across this country, to have one [a professional standards board] in every state. It is an appointment by the governor to serve. There are particular constituency groups listed in the law. And so it's a very deliberate group that looks at certification and continuing education and programs which help new teachers be successful.*

The board wanted professional growth training as an absolute must for every teacher, mandated in the school level. I thought that there wasn't really funding to do that, to adopt standardized training for them. And I really wanted to put a system in place that would design improvement from the systemic approach. And so I was able to entice some people who were very knowledgeable to work on this committee. I had no clue at all what we should do.

So I helped facilitate that group coming up with a really great system. Now it's not in place yet; so this is just the second year of its pilot. But in this the teacher can work on [a] core improvement team, can use a colleague as a practitioner in helping them look at their teaching, and at their goals. It's based on the student standards of Indiana; it's based on the teachers' standards and the developmental standards. You are to develop your goals, professional goals for the activities that you do, which need to impact student achievement. That doesn't mean that has to be measured by a certain amount of student achievement; it just means you need to know what outcome you have had with your curricula with regards to your students. And make that a part of your reflective piece.

And that's exciting. 'Cause in the past you knew you would get six hours of college credit and then with very little—not that the courses were bad, but it oftentimes didn't have a connection to what you actually did in the classroom. And this system is built on your actual teaching. There will be alternate ways, and alternative ways to do it for people who don't really have a classroom. If they are coming back from a leave, they need six hours to fulfill the requirement. But it is a self-improvement plan; it's called Professional Growth Plan. It's not huge, and it's not like a portfolio project. And the original design was a portfolio project, and I wanted that whatever our committee did, for it to be meaningful and also doable. And that's what I think we did.

In 1981 Cordell Affeldt delivered thousands of "oars" to Governor Robert Orr, inscribed with messages from participants at Save Our School rallies. Left to right: Affeldt, Dale Harris, Don Hogan, Nancy Papas, Roger Williams, Norma Kacen and Robert Margraf. ISTA Archives.

Although strikes decreased markedly in number and duration after the implementation of PL217, they did not cease altogether; teachers for ECTA (Elkhart Classroom Teachers Association) struck in 1985. ISTA Archives.

In 1991 teachers gathered in front of the statehouse to urge immediate action on the state's budget. However, it took a special session to resolve the budget that year. ISTA Archives.

President-elect Judith Briganti posed with her fourth grade class in Elkhart, Indiana, in 2001. Since the office became a fulltime position, presidents generally have taken a leave of absence from their school systems during their tenure. ISTA Archives.

ISTA's History Task Force was formed in 1996 to oversee the 150th anniversary celebration of the Association. Front row, left to right: John Ransford; Sarah Borgman; Donita Mize, chairperson; Dorothy Short; and Gene Price. Second row: Mattie Miller; Linda Weintraut, writer; Bob Barcus, consultant; and Jack Spindler. ISTA Archives.

Epilogue

An Unfinished Agenda

At the end of the 1987 legislative session, the lobbying team of the Indiana State Teachers Association lamented that it had not achieved its goals; ISTA and education in Indiana were left with "an unfinished agenda." Indeed, it had been a difficult year for the Association as Governor Robert Orr had pushed his reform program through the General Assembly. During such daily struggles, it was easy to feel disappointed. However, had the lobbying team reflected on the history of the organization, perhaps their minds would have been eased by the great strides that had been made by the Indiana State Teachers Association.

In retrospect, much has been accomplished in 150 years. In 1854, the first year of the Association, many Hoosiers had doubted the need for formal education at all; yet by 2003 every Hoosier took for granted the promise of the state constitution of free public education for all students. Along the way, teachers, parents, and the general public came to understand that every child should have access to public education and that the state benefited when children and adolescents were required to attend school. Citizens no longer questioned the need for "a competent corps of instructors" or the need for students to be educated in an adequately appointed, comfortable classroom.

A strong organization of individuals had helped guide such achievements. Personalities such as Caleb Mills, Abram Shortridge, Belle O'Hair, and especially Robert Wyatt made an indelible imprint upon the Association and the face of public education. In the process education became less a force of civic responsibility and more an agent of social reform. In effect, the efforts of these educators helped change the face of American society. It had been social reform that set the organization in motion, made universal public education a reality, and modernized and consolidated schools. Then it was reformers who initiated the transformation of ISTA into a union in the 1970s when teachers' rights became the driving force.

Amazingly, however, with all of the changes over the course of 150 years, some things had not changed. Teachers still fought for increased pay, and citizens still called for remedies to the poor state of Indiana's educational system. Educators and bureaucrats still debated "who would set the standards for the teaching profession." The new generation of leaders of ISTA, the people who would guide it in the twenty-first century, still faced the recurring struggles for control of the process of public education in Indiana, and they still faced the ubiquitous struggle for funding. In the new century, members of the teaching profession also were addressing new challenges: the use of technology in the classroom, distance learning, financial stability for the organization, the impact of vouchers and charter schools, student threats of violence on the Internet, and increasing needs for school response plans and security systems, as well as new legal issues.

Advancing the cause of education has become an increasingly complex endeavor. In this, ISTA's 150th year, the Association is more than just "an organized body of efficient educators" who come together to learn about educational issues and to set forth an agenda for lobbying—although those remain central efforts. Since the 1970s ISTA has functioned as a labor union, furthering its cause through the use of the strike and collective bargaining. It offers membership services that include leadership training, insurance, and job placement. And with the construction of its state headquarters building in the 1950s and its remodeling in the 1980s, ISTA is a significant physical presence in the capital city.

Indeed, ISTA has become many things to its growing membership. It now boasts 273 affiliates and 137 employees. Its mission statement reflects a shift in emphasis; no longer does it act for the membership but now provides the means to allow them to act. Now the primary focus is "to provide the resources necessary to enable local affiliates to advocate effectively for members and for public education." Yes, the Association given form by Caleb Mills 150 years ago has evolved. Still, even in its evolution, education and the issues of children have remained key to the viability of the Association. Over the past 150 years, members of ISTA have endeavored "to advance the cause of education." Much has been accomplished. Nevertheless, with such an agenda, there is always much more to do.

Notes

Notes to Introduction

1. United States Bureau of the Census, Decennial Census (1840).

2. "At the First Teachers' Association, Indianapolis, 1854," *Indianapolis Star Magazine,* October 5, 1919.

3. Ibid.

4. Ibid.

5. Ibid.

6. Ibid.

7. Justin E. Walsh, *The Centennial History of the Indiana General Assembly, 1816–1978* (Indianapolis: Indiana Historical Bureau, 1987), 142.

Notes to Chapter I

1. "Beginnings of Indiana Teacher's Organization," *Indianapolis News,* December 29, 1904.

2. Petitioning, later referred to as lobbying, became an accepted and formalized procedure that was used to influence the actions of the legislature toward a desired goal.

3. Glenda Riley, *Divorce: An American Tradition* (New York: Oxford University Press, 1991), 65; David McCulloch, *John Adams* (New York: Simon & Schuster, 2001), 104.

4. Theda Skopol, *Protecting Soldiers and Mothers: The Political Origins of Social Policy in the United States* (Cambridge: The Belknap Press of Harvard University Press, 1992), 90.

5. Donald F. Carmony, *Indiana, 1816–1850: The Pioneer Era* (Indianapolis: Indiana Historical Society, 1998), 363, 369.

6. United States Bureau of the Census, *Decennial Census* (1840).

7. James H. Madison, *Indiana through Tradition and Change: A History of the Hoosier State and Its People* (Indianapolis: Indiana Historical Society, 1982), 111, 113; Emma Lou Thornbrough, *Indiana in the Civil War Period, 1850–1880* (Indianapolis: Indiana Historical Bureau and Indiana Historical Society, 1965), 461; "Report of the Committee on Education," *Indiana Common School Report 1843–51,* Indiana Division, Indiana State Library, Indianapolis.

8. Carmony, *The Pioneer Era,* 369–75.

9. Ibid., 375.

10. Ibid., 377.

11. Thomas Clinton Pears, Jr., *New Harmony: An Adventure in Happiness, Papers of Thomas and Sarah Pears* (Indianapolis: Indiana Historical Society, 1933), 16.

12. Walsh, *Centennial History,* 141.

13. Charles W. Moores, *Caleb Mills and Indiana School System* (Indianapolis: Indiana Historical Society, 1905), 386, 387.

14. William O. Lynch, "The Great Awakening," *Indiana Magazine of History* 41 (June 1945): 108.

15. Moores, *Caleb Mills,* 388.

16. Thornbrough, *Indiana in the Civil War Era,* 465.

17. Lynch, "The Great Awakening," 111.

18. "100 Years of Progress in Education," *Indianapolis Star Magazine*, October 17, 1954.

19. "At the First Teachers Association, Indianapolis, 1854," *Indianapolis Star Magazine*, October 15, 1919.

20. "The State Teachers Association," *Indianapolis Star*, October 14, 1920.

21. Thornbrough, *Indiana in the Civil War Era,* 470; *Decennial Census*, 1850.

22. "The State Teachers Association," *Indianapolis Star*, October 14, 1920.

23. Warren F. Collins, "A History of the Indiana State Teachers' Association" (MA thesis, Indiana University, 1926), 36.

24. "100 Years of Progress in Education," *Indianapolis Star Magazine*, October 17, 1954.

25. Thornbrough, *Indiana in the Civil War Era,* 474; Collins, "History," 37.

26. "Influence of the War upon Education," *Indiana School Journal* 6 (1861): 194.

27. Thornbrough, *Indiana in the Civil War Era,* 474.

Notes to Chapter II

1. William O. Lynch, "The Great Awakening," *Indiana Magazine of History* 41 (June 1945): 113.

2. James H. Madison, *The Indiana Way: A State History* (Indianapolis: Indiana Historical Society and Indiana University Press, 1986), 114, 147.

3. Michael B. Katz, *In the Shadow of the Poorhouse: A Social History of Welfare in America* (New York: Basic Books, 1996), 135–37; David I. Macleod, *The Age of the Child: Children in America, 1890–1920* (New York: Twayne Publishers, 1998), 87–88.

4. Robert B. Robinson and Ana Marie Wahl, "Industrial Employment and Wages of Women, Men, and Children in a 19th Century City: Indianapolis, 1850–1880," *American Sociological Review* 55 (December 1990): 912–28.

5. Macleod, *Age of the Child*, 1–14, 139–40. Macleod talks about how the ideal of the "economically 'worthless' but emotionally 'priceless' child," already integral to the new model middle-class family, came to pervade urban culture, 14.

6. Emma Lou Thornbrough, *Indiana in the Civil War Era* (Indianapolis: Indiana Historical Bureau and Indiana Historical Society, 1965), 475–76; Madison, *The Indiana Way*, 181; Macleod, *Age of Child*, 79.

7. Thornbrough, *Indiana in the Civil War Era*, 478–79; David J. Bodenhamer and Robert G. Barrows, eds., *The Encyclopedia of Indianapolis* (Bloomington: Indiana University Press, 1994), 1259.

8. "Editorial Miscellany," *Indiana School Journal* 5 (1860): 135.

9. Macleod, *Age of Child*, 79.

10. Madison, *The Indiana Way*, 181, 188; Thornbrough, *Indiana in the Civil War Era*, 478.

11. J. N. Hurty, "Sanitary Conditions in Our School-Houses," *The Inland Educator* 7 (1898): 9.

12. "100 Years of Progress in Education," *Indianapolis Star Magazine*, October 17, 1954.

13. Ledger, *Minutes of the Indiana Teachers' Association, 1896–1907,* 568.

14. Thornbrough, *Indiana in the Civil War Era,* 481–82.

15. "Resolution from the Annual Meeting of ISTA," *Indiana School Journal* 10 (1864): 55.

16. Thornbrough, *Indiana in the Civil War*, 482–83.

17. Madison, *The Indiana Way*, 181, 183.

18. "100 Years," *Indianapolis Star Magazine*, October 17, 1954; J. Clifton Phillips, *Indiana in Transition: The Emergence of an Industrial Commonwealth, 1880–1920* (Indianapolis: Indiana Historical Bureau and Indiana Historical Society), 389.

19. Phillips, *Indiana in Transition*, 399.

20. Ibid., 389, 395; L. M. Campbell Adams, "An Investigation of Housing and Living Conditions in Three Districts in Indianapolis," *Indiana University Studies* 8 (September 1910): 133–35.

21. This information is contained in many Indiana history books; see James H. Madison's *The Indiana Way*, 150.

Notes to Chapter III

1. *Indiana School Journal* 1 (1856): 13.

2. Warren F. Collins, "A History of the Indiana State Teachers' Association" (MA Thesis, Indiana University, 1926), 46.

3. "A Short Plea for Teachers' Associations," *Indiana School Journal* 5 (1860): 135; State of Indiana, Department of Public Instruction, *19th Biennial Report of the State Superintendent* (July 31, 1897– July 31, 1898): 307, 315.

4. "Editorial Miscellany," *Indiana School Journal* 5 (1860): 310; "Resolution of the State Teachers' Association," *Indiana School Journal* 21 (1876): 88.

5. *Indiana School Journal* 1 (1856).

6. *19th Biennial Report*, 685; "Teachers' Reading Circle Books," *Indiana School Journal* 41 (1896): 519.

7. "Editorial Miscellany," *Indiana School Journal* 18 (1873): 132.

8. Ibid.

9. "Editorial Miscellany," *Indiana School Journal* 8 (1863): 298.

10. "Editorial Miscellany," *Indiana School Journal* 5 (1860): 310; James H. Madison, *Indiana through Tradition and Change: A History of the Hoosier State and Its People* (Indianapolis: Indiana Historical Society, 1982), 275; Ledger, *Minutes of the Annual Meetings, Indiana State Teachers' Association 1896–1907*, 19.

11. "The State Teachers' Association," *Indiana School Journal* 3 (1858): 17–18; Clifton J. Phillips, *Indiana in Transition: The Emergence of an Industrial Commonwealth, 1880–1920* (Indianapolis: Indiana Historical Bureau and Indiana Historical Society, 1968), 419; "Teachers Begin Hot Campaign for Higher Standard of Wages," *Indianapolis Journal*, December 31, 1903.

12. Phillips, *Indiana in Transition*, 406–07.

13. "Our Minimum Wage," *Indiana Teacher* 69 (1924): 13.

14. "Editorial Miscellany," *Indiana School Journal* 11 (1866): 30; "Shall Teachers Be Pensioned?" *Indiana School Journal* 21 (1876): 477.

15. "Shall Teachers Be Pensioned?" *Indiana School Journal* 21 (1876): 477; "Join to Aid Infirm and Aged Teachers," *Indianapolis Star*, December 23, 1910; "100 Years of Progress in Education," *Indianapolis Star Magazine*, October 17, 1954; Phillips, *Indiana in Transition*, 407.

16. Board of Trustees of the Retirement Fund, "Indiana State Teachers' Retirement Fund, Bulletin of Information Regarding the Retirement Law, As Amended by the Law of 1937–1939," 1940, Indiana Division, Indiana State Library, Indianapolis.

17. "Should the Indiana Legislature Favor Teacher Tenure?" *Indiana Teacher* 69 (1924–25): 20; Madison, *Tradition and Change,* 276.

Notes to Chapter IV

1. David I. Macleod, *The Age of the Child: Children in America, 1890–1920* (New York: Twayne Publishers, 1998), 80–84.

2. Letter, October 1917, Correspondence, vol. 13, Indiana State Council of Defense, Indiana State Archives, Indianapolis.

3. Clifton J. Phillips, *Indiana in Transition: The Emergence of an Industrial Commonwealth, 1880–1920* (Indianapolis: Indiana Historical Bureau and Indiana Historical Society, 1968), 399; Macleod, *Age of the Child,* 85; Arthur Zilversmit, *Changing Schools: Progressive Education Theory and Practice, 1930–1960* (Chicago: University of Chicago Press, 1993), 2; "Complete Report of the General Association," *The Educator Journal* 10 (1909–10): 293.

4. Indiana Department of Public Instruction Study, *Why Does Indiana Rank 17?* 1920; State of Indiana, Indiana Education Survey Commission, *Public Education in Indiana* (New York: General Education Commission, 1923): v–x.

5. James H. Madison, *Indiana through Tradition and Change: A History of the Hoosier State and Its People* (Indianapolis: Indiana Historical Society, 1982), 267; *Public Education in Indiana,* 15.

6. Madison, *Tradition and Change,* 267.

7. *Public Education in Indiana,* 144.

8. Ibid., 140–44.

9. Macleod, *Age of the Child,* 86.

10. "Teachers Pick Local Woman as Chief," *Indianapolis Star,* October 21, 1922; Lara P. Good, "Teachers' Contract," Blackford County, Indiana (1914); "Miss Wilson Is Elected," *Indianapolis Star,* October 31, 1915.

11. "Miss Wilson Is Elected," *Indianapolis Star,* October 31, 1915.

12. "Teachers Pick Local Woman as Chief," *Indianapolis Star,* October 21, 1922.

13. "A Township Trustee on the County Unit," *Indiana Teacher* 69 (1924–25): 23, 24, 26; "Teachers Pick Local Woman as Chief," *Indianapolis Star,* October 21, 1922.

14. Madison, *Tradition and Change,* 271.

15. Ibid., 265–74.

16. Linda Weintraut, "The Limits of 'Enlightened Self-Interest': Business Power in Indianapolis, 1900–1977" (Ph.D. diss., Indiana University, 2001): 130–35.

17. Ibid.

18. Bodenhamer and Barrows, eds., *The Encyclopedia of Indianapolis*, 481–83; Madison, *Tradition and Change*, 280.

19. "Indiana Teachers Choose Officers," *Indianapolis News*, October 31, 1914.

20. "15,000 Teachers in Session Here: Fight New Plan," *Indianapolis Star*, October 21, 1921.

21. Ibid.; Executive Committee, Minutes, December 2, 1922.

22. Executive Committee, Minutes, December 2, 1922.

23. *Indianapolis Star*, September 14, 1938.

24. "State Teachers' Leader Decries Unequal Burden," *Indianapolis Star*, October 21, 1932.

25. "Teachers Plan Merged Front in Tax Defense," *Indianapolis Star*, October 20, 1934; Madison, *Tradition and Change,* 283.

26. "The Sales Tax," *Indiana Teacher* 78 (March 1933): 12.

27. "Indiana's Teachers Expect Fight over Income Law," *Indianapolis Star*, October 19, 1934.

28. "Its Leadership," *Indiana Teacher* 79 (January 1934): 14.

29. Board of Trustees of the Retirement Fund, "Indiana State Teachers' Retirement Fund, Bulletin of Information Regarding the Retirement Law, As Amended by the Law of 1937–1939," 1940, Indiana State Library, Indianapolis.

30. "Forward," *Indiana Teacher* 79 (October 1934): 18.

31. Ibid.

32. "Editorial," *Indiana Teacher* 78 (March 1933): 15.

33. "Charles O. Williams," *Indianapolis News*, September 14, 1938.

34. "Teachers' Group Secretary Dies," *Indianapolis Star*, September 14, 1938.

Notes to Chapter V

1. "Secretary's Page-Annual Report of Secretary," *Indiana Teacher* 84 (1939–40): 20.

2. "Memorial in Retrospect," Indiana State Teachers Association, n.d.

3. Robert H. Wyatt, interview by Randell W. Jehs, Indiana State Library Oral History Project (1972–75): 1–3.

4. Speech by Robert H. Wyatt, May 10, 1973, Indiana State Teachers Association, Indianapolis, Indiana.

5. Madison, *Tradition and Change*, 394; *Indianapolis Star*, October 22, 1942; *Indianapolis Star*, October 23, 1941.

6. Madison, *Tradition and Change*, 394; "Report of Research Director," *Indiana Teacher* 89 (1944–45): 34; "Teachers Open Scholarship Fund," *Indianapolis News*, February 6, 1946.

7. *Laws of the State of Indiana*, 1943: 355.

8. Wyatt interview, 37; "Memorial in Retrospect," n. p.; *Laws of the State of Indiana*, 2, 1945:1529–1531.

9. Wyatt interview, 86–88.

10. Ibid.

11. Walsh, *Centennial History*, 594.

12. "Report of Research Director," *Indiana Teacher* 92 (1947–48): 46.

13. Weintraut, "The Limits of Enlightened Self-Interest," 191–93.

14. "Annual Report of the Executive Secretary," *Indiana Teacher* 93 (1948–49): 41.

15. Ibid.

16. "Annual Report of the Executive Secretary," *Indiana Teacher* 95 (1950–51): 39.

17. "Report of the Field Service and Placement Director," *Indiana Teacher* 92 (1947–48): 47; "Annual Report of the Executive Secretary," *Indiana Teacher* 93 (1948–49): 39.

18. "The Job Ahead," *Indiana Teacher* 101 (1956–57): 58.

19. Wyatt interview, 49.

20. "News," *Indiana Teacher* 95 (1950–51): 19; Speech by Robert H. Wyatt, May 10, 1973, Indiana State Teachers Association, Indianapolis, Indiana.

21. "17,000 Hoosier Teachers Ready for Convention," *Indianapolis Star*, October 21, 1953; "Teachers to run Meetings as a Legislature," *Indianapolis News*, October 28, 1953; "Teachers Convention to be on TV, Radio," *Indianapolis Times*, October 21, 1953.

22. "The Representative Assembly," *Indiana Teacher* 96 (1951–52): 14–15.

23. "The Job Ahead," *Indiana Teacher* 101 (1956–57): 58.

24. Ibid.

25. "Pay-As-You-Go," *Indiana Teacher* 101 (1956–57): 194; "Teachers Dunned for New Building," *Indianapolis News*, March 25, 1956.

26. "Teachers Beat Plan to Raise Dues $55," *Indianapolis News,* October 25, 1963; "$55 ISTA Building Assessment Sought," *Indianapolis Star,* October 16, 1963; "ISTA Will Debate Plea for $5 Boost," *Indianapolis News,* October 20, 1964; "Stahl Elected ISTA Chief Unanimously," *Indianapolis News,* October 22, 1964.

27. "9-Story Teachers Building to Be Completed June 15," *Indianapolis News*, April 24, 1958.

28. *Indiana Teacher* 102 (October 1958): 54.

Notes to Chapter VI

1. Wyatt interview, 121.

2. *Indianapolis News,* October 24, 1941.

3. Joe Alex Morris, "They Don't Want Uncle's Money," *Saturday Evening Post,* March 22, 1952, 30–31, 141–42, 144.

4. Weintraut, "The Limits of Enlightened Self-Interest," 54–103.

5. Weintraut, "Enlightened Self-Interest," 54–100; Alan Brinkley, *Unfinished Nation: A Concise History of the American People, II* (New York: McGraw Hill, 1993), 766.

6. M. J. Heale, *American Anti-Communism: Combating the Enemy Within, 1830–1970* (Baltimore, Md: Johns Hopkins University Press, 1990), 184–87; Zilversmit, *Changing Schools,* 146.

7. Zilversmit, *Changing Schools,* 2–3.

8. "A Message to the Teachers of Indiana," *Indiana Teacher* 95 (1950–51): 62.

9. Ibid., 63.

10. *Indianapolis News,* November 8, 1950.

11. "Let Us Invite Criticism of the Schools," *Indiana Teacher* 96 (1951–52): 120.

12. Ibid.

13. Zilversmit, *Changing Schools,* 103–06.

14. "Let Us Invite Criticism of the Schools," *Indiana Teacher* 96 (1951–52): 120.

15. "Are We 'The Enemy?'" *Indianapolis Star,* January 31, 1952.

16. Heale, *American Anti-Communism,* 184.

17. "The United States Supreme Court Acts," *Indiana Teacher* 96 (1951–52): 244–55.

18. "Who's Trying to Ruin Our Schools?" *Indiana Teacher* 96 (1951–52): 150.

19. "Magruder Scratched from Eligible List for at Least 5 Years," *Indianapolis Times,* December 11, 1952.

20. Wyatt interview, 117.

21. "Raps Teachers for Spread of Socialism," *Indianapolis Times,* December 12, 1952.

22. "Teacher Poll Proposal Hit," *Indianapolis Star,* November 26, 1952; Weintraut, "Enlightened Self-Interest," 194–95; "Socialist Link Charged to Teachers' Speaker," *Indianapolis Star,* October 25, 1952.

23. "Ban 'Robin Hood' as Red Bait, urges Text Prober," *Indianapolis Times,* November 12, 1953; "Critic Doesn't Know Her Quakers, Educator Says"; "Sher-

iff in Robin's Lair Vows Bandit No Red," *Indianapolis News*, November 14, 1953; "'Robin Hood' Called Red Propaganda Tool; Sherwood Forest Folk Defend Storybook Hero," *Louisville Courier Journal*, November 14, 1953; "'Robin Was a Hood but Surely No Red,'" *Indianapolis News*, November 14, 1953. "Book Banning Idea Denied," *Indianapolis Star,* February 2, 1955; "Red Fighter is Really an Average Housewife," *Indianapolis Times*, March 20, 1955.

24. *Indianapolis Times*, August 11, 1953.

25. "ISTA's Just Bustin' Out All Over,'" *Indiana Teacher* 98 (1953–54): 51.

26. "Editorial Notes to Teachers," *Indiana Teacher* 98 (1953–54): 151–52; "Can't Teachers Hear Both Sides?" *Indianapolis Star*, October 24, 1953.

27. *Indianapolis Star*, October 22, 1954.

28. Zilversmit, *Changing Schools*, 115; David Halberstam, *The Fifties* (New York: Fawcett Columbine, 1993), 6.

29. *Indianapolis Star*, October 18, 1959.

30. Weintraut, "Enlightened Self-Interest," 173; Brinkley, *Unfinished Nation*, 789.

31. Wyatt interview, 121.

32. Allen J. Matusow, *The Unraveling of America: A History of Liberalism in the 1960s* (New York: Harper & Row, 1984), 221.

Notes to Chapter VII

1. *Indianapolis Times,* December 7, 1958.

2. Wyatt interview, 168.

3. Justin E. Walsh, *The Centennial History of the Indiana General Assembly, 1816–1978* (Indianapolis: Indiana Historical Bureau, 1987), 594.

4. Ibid.; Robert Margraf, oral history interview with John Warner, July 14, 2000.

5. *Indianapolis Star*, October 5, 1952; George Brown Tindell, *America: A Narrative History, I* (New York: W. W. Norton & Company, 1992), 1285; *Indianapolis Times*, October 24, 1957.

6. "Indiana Democrats Molding 1954 Platform Urged to Help Schools," *Monticello Herald-Tribune*, June 4, 1954; "Democrats Told of School Needs," *Indianapolis Times*, June 4, 1954; "Federal Aid to Education," *Elwood Call*, June 12, 1954; "New Method of Financing of School Buildings," *Columbia City Commercial Mail*, September 8, 1954; "Further Aid to Schools Opposed by C. of C.," *Indianapolis Star,* September 30, 1954; "Keep Our Schools Local," *Muncie Star*, October 27, 1954.

7. "Johnson Elected ISTA President," *Indianapolis Star*, October 24, 1958.

8. Madison, *Indiana Way*, 250.

9. *Indianapolis Star*, October 27, 1968.

10. "Bobbitt Defeat Commented on by Bar Leader," *Indianapolis Star*, November 13, 1962.

11. Ibid.; "To Keep Justice Just," *Indianapolis Star*, November 26, 1962; "Do Teachers Have a Right to Vote," *Indianapolis Times*, November 14, 1962.

12. Tindall, *America*, 1389; Alan Brinkley, *Unfinished Nation: A Concise History of the American People, II* (New York: McGraw Hill, 1993), 837–83; James Miller, *Democracy Is in the Streets: From Port Huron to the Siege of Chicago* (New York: Simon & Schuster, 1989), 13–14; Todd Gitlin, *The Sixties: Years of Hope, Days of Rage* (New York: Bantam, 1987), 27.

13. *Indianapolis News*, October 16, 1965; *Indianapolis News*, October 22, 1967; *Indianapolis Star*, October 21, 1968; *Indianapolis News*, November 16, 1969; John Ransford, oral history interview with John Warner, July 27, 2000.

14. *Indianapolis Star*, October 21, 1968.

15. "Nation Looks to Schools to Heal Social Wounds," *Indiana Teacher* 113 (Fall 1968): 10.

16. Ibid.; *Indianapolis Star*, May 26, 1968.

17. Robert Barcus, oral history interview with Linda Weintraut, August 3, 2000.

18. Ibid.

19. Ibid.

20. "Editorial," *Indiana Teacher* 115 (Winter 1970): 62

21. *Indiana Teacher* 69 (October 1924): 18; *Laws of the State of Indiana*, 1921: 751.

22. *Indianapolis News*, September 14, 1938.

23. *Indianapolis News*, June 27, 1969.

24. *Journal and Courier*, October 10, 1971; "Wyatt Pension Gets Attention of Prosecutor," *Muncie Evening Press,* October 19, 1971; "Wants to Hear Tapes About Wyatt's Pension," *Bedford Daily Times-Mail*, October 20, 1971; "Task Force Seeks Tapes Dealing with Wyatt's Pension," *The Elkhart Truth*, October 19, 1971.

25. *Indianapolis News*, June 25, 1984.

Notes to Chapter VIII

1. Any number of general histories discuss the evolution from peacetime protest to violence. Todd Gitlin, *The Sixties: Years of Hope, Days of Rage* (New York: Bantam, 1987), and Alan Matusow, *The Unraveling of America: A History of Liberalism in the 1960s* (New York: Harper & Row, 1984) are representative.

2. "Wyatt Resigns Indiana Teacher Executive Post," *Indianapolis News*, April 29, 1971.

3. "Jensen Says ISTA's Needs Changing," *Indianapolis News*, January 7, 1972.

4. John Ransford, oral history interview with John Warner, July 27, 2000; Joanna Hock, response to questionnaire, 2000, Indiana State Teachers Association Archives, Indianapolis.

5. Indiana State Teachers Association, *Indiana State Teachers Association Handbook*, 1970, 1971, 1975–76, Indiana State Teachers Association Archives, Indianapolis.

6. Hock questionnaire.

7. Ransford interview; J. David Young, oral history interview with Linda Weintraut, July 18, 2000.

8. *Handbook*, 1970, 77; *Handbook*, 1975–76, 42.

9. "Jensen Says ISTA's Needs Changing," *Indianapolis News,* January 7, 1972.

10. Ibid.

11. Susan Lowell Butler, *The National Education Association: A Special Mission* (New York: NEA, 1987), 72.

12. Samuel L. Blumenfeld, *NEA Trojan Horse in American Education* (Boise, Idaho: Paradigm Company, 1984), 79, 203.

13. Budgets of the Indiana State Teachers Association, 1976–88, Files of the Indiana State Teachers Association, Indiana State Teachers Association Archives, Indianapolis.

14. "Working for You," *Teacher Advocate* II (September 1973): 10.

15. Damon Moore, oral history interview with John Warner, July 27, 2000; Ransford interview.

16. Robert Margraf, interview with John Warner, July 14, 2000; Budget for Indiana State Teachers Association, 1988, Files of the Indiana State Teachers Association, Indiana State Teachers Association Archives, Indianapolis.

17. "ISTA Extends Jensen's Contract," *Indianapolis Star,* March 18, 1973; *Handbook,* 1971–76.

18. "6 Are Named to ISTA Staff Positions," *Indianapolis Star,* June 14, 1972; "Co-Ordinator for Teacher Activities, Services Named," *Indianapolis Star,* September 10, 1972.

19. Hock questionnaire.

20. "ISTA-ICTA Merger," *Teacher Advocate* II (September 1973): 1; "Teachers Unit Votes to Merge with ISTA," *Indianapolis Star,* August 26, 1973.

21. "History of the Indiana State Federation of Public School Teachers," unpublished, 1951.

22. Ibid.; Robert Hall Wyatt, interview by Randell W. Jehs, Indiana State Library Oral History Project (1972–75): 1–3.

23. "ISTA-ICTA Merger," *Teacher Advocate* II (September 1973): 1, 6.

24. Young, oral history interview with Linda Weintraut.

Notes to Chapter IX

1. "Does Bargaining Make a Difference? One Case Study," *ISTA Advocate* XIX (April–May 1991): 10.

2. Indiana State Teachers Association, "Collective Bargaining Law, 25th Year Commemorative," 12.

3. Ibid.; Warren Williams, oral history interview with Linda Weintraut, July 20, 2000.

4. Samuel L. Blumenfeld, *NEA Trojan Horse in American Education* (Boise, Idaho: Paradigm Company), 139–49.

5. Ibid., 2.

6. Robert Margraf, oral history interview with John Warner, July 14, 2000, September 21, 2000.

7. 25th Year Commemorative, 2.

8. Ibid.

9. Margraf, oral history interview with John Warner.

10. "Highland Teachers Stay on the Line," *Teacher Advocate* II (October 1973): 3.

11. "Suit Filed for Highland Five," *Teacher Advocate* II (February 1974): 15; J. David Young, oral history interview with Linda Weintraut, July 18, 2000.

12. "Report Urges ISTA to Improve Planning," *Indianapolis Star,* April 11, 1973.

13. "Proceedings of the Representative Assembly, October 1973," 16, Indiana State Teachers Association Archives, Indianapolis.

14. "25th Year Commemorative," 3.

15. "Proceedings Representative Assembly, May 1974," 32, Indiana State Teachers Association Archives, Indianapolis.

16. "School Boards Unveil Strike Plan," *Teacher Advocate* III (April 1975): 1.

17. Ibid.

18. "Two Views on Collective Bargaining," *Teacher Advocate* III (January 1975): 13.

19. "Teachers' Chief Pushes Law for Right to Strike," *Indianapolis Star,* January 11, 1978.

20. "Agency Shop—Some Questions Answered," *Teacher Advocate* III (June 1975): 10.

21. Budgets for Indiana State Teachers Association, 1978–88, Files of the Indiana State Teachers Association, Indiana State Teachers Association Archives, Indianapolis; Robert Barcus, oral history interview with Linda Weintraut and John Warner, August 3, 2000.

22. "Who's in Charge Here or A Case for Due Process," *Teacher Advocate* III (June 1975): 8.

23. Ibid.

24. "Now Is the Time to Fire Teachers," *Teacher Advocate* VI (May 1978): 1.

25. State of Indiana, *Acts of 1991, 107th Indiana General Assembly, Volume III*: 2389.

26. *Marion Chronicle-Tribune,* August 28, 1978–September 8, 1978.

27. "RACT Offers Binding Arbitration," *Richmond Palladium-Item*, August 28, 1978.

28. "Teacher Strike Ends," *Richmond Palladium-Item*, September 6, 1978.

29. Robert Margraf, oral history interview with John Warner, July 14, 2000; Sarah Borgman, oral history interview with Linda Weintraut, July 28, 2000.

Notes to Chapter X

1. "ISTA: A Powerhouse in Statehouse," *Indianapolis Star*, February 7, 1988.

2. "We Have Arrived," *ISTA Advocate* XI (January–February 1983): 2.

3. Questions are invariably raised about the departure of non-teacher's from ISTA in the mid-1970s; the author interviewed four retired superintendents telephonically in late February and early March 2003. One individual Ted Hughes recalled a memo in 1969 or 1970 from Robert Wyatt that stated, "superintendents were no longer welcome in ISTA." Three interviewees, Ken Koger, Charles Fields, and J. R. Johnson did not recollect any letter, memo, or note on this subject. From their comments, however, two other reasons for the exodus appear possible. Ideologically, superintendents and administrators found themselves relegated to a secondary level of membership as management policies in ISTA changed—once teachers gained control of the organization, they refused to relinquish any amount of their recently acquired, hard-won power to superintendents, principals, or administrators. Also, see Wyatt interview 295–296.

4. *Indianapolis Star*, February 2, 1973; *Indianapolis News*, April 20, 1973; Telephone call with Charles Fields on March 13, 2003.

5. "IPACE for Impact through Political Action," *Teacher Advocate* II (January 1974): 8.

6. Robert Barcus, oral history interview with Linda Weintraut and John Warner, August 3, 2000.

7. "The Bargaining Law, Now . . . ," *Teacher Advocate* I (June 1973): 6.

8. Robert Margraf, oral history interview with John Warner, July 14, 2000.

9. Robert Margraf, oral history interview with John Warner, September 21, 2000.

10. "I-PACE: Off and Running," *Teacher Advocate* II (April 1974): 11.

11. "ISTA Organ Calls Election 'Finest Hour' for Teachers," *Indianapolis Star*, November 24, 1974.

12. "I-PACE for Impact through Political Action," *Teacher Advocate* II (January 1974): 8.

13. "We Have Arrived," *ISTA Advocate* XI (January–February 1983): 2, 4.

14. Ibid.; "It's 'Presidents Plus Two' for Legislative Action," *Teacher Advocate* 8 (January–February 1980): 1.

15. "Teachers Rally at Home, Lobby in Washington to SAVE OUR SCHOOLS," *Teacher Advocate* IX (May 1981): 7; Alan Brinkley, *Unfinished Nation: A Concise History of the American People, II* (New York: McGraw Hill, 1993), 882–84.

16. "March to Support Education Planned," *ISTA Advocate* X (December 1981): 5.

17. "Rally at Home . . .," *Teacher Advocate* IX (May 1981): 6.

18. Ibid.; Sarah Borgman, oral history interview with Linda Weintraut, July 28, 2000.

19. "Teachers Go Back to School on World of Politics," *ISTA Advocate* XII (September 1983): 5.

20. "RA Okays 'Options Guaranteed,'" *ISTA Advocate* XIII (December 1984): 4.

21. "An Interview with ISTA's Outgoing President," *ISTA Advocate* XII (August 1983): 4.

22. "RA Okays 'Options Guaranteed,'" *ISTA Advocate* XIII (December 1984): 4.

23. "Schools Are Not Improving Study Says," *Indianapolis Star,* February 28, 1994.

24. "1984 Indiana Legislature Sputters to a Close," *ISTA Advocate* 12 (March 1984): 5; "ISTA's Legislative Stand: No Excellence without Investments," *ISTA Advocate* (January/February 1985): 6; "Various Public Education Programs Enacted and Funded by the Indiana General Assembly," July 1, 1983–June 30, 1997, Indiana State Teachers Association Archives, Indianapolis.

25. "Indiana's Top School Official Surveys Controversies," *ISTA Advocate* XIII (August 1984): 6.

26. "ISTA Supports Higher Standards," *Indianapolis News*, March 2, 1983.

27. "Let's Match Solutions to Problems," *ISTA Advocate* XV (March 1987): 2.

28. "ISTEP Survey Results," *ISTA Advocate* XVII (August 1988): 3.

29. "ISTA's Legislative Stand: No Excellence without Investments," *ISTA Advocate* XIII (January/February 1985): 7.

30. National Education Association, *Separating the Wheat from the Chaff: How Much Do Schools Really Benefit When States Raise Taxes on Their Behalf?* (Washington, D.C.: NEA, 1996), 6.

31. "Teacher Evaluation: Does It Measure Up?" *ISTA Advocate* XII (March 1984): 9.

32. Ibid.

33. "Orr and Evans Defend A+ Program," *ISTA Advocate* XVI (October 1987): 6, 7; "ISTEP Seals State Domination of Curriculum," *ISTA Advocate* XVI (April 1988): 2.

34. "It's Our Profession," *ISTA Advocate* XV (January/February 1987): 2.

35. "Robert Margraf's Legacy to Public Education and ISTA Members," *Indianapolis News*, January 7, 1988.

36. Ibid.; J. David Young, oral history interview with Linda Weintraut, July 18, 2000; "Our ISTA at 140 Years," Remarks to Representative Assembly by Garrett L. Harbron, October 22, 1994.

37. "Teachers Union Shores up for House Lobbying," *Indianapolis Star*, February 3, 1995.

38. "Teachers Union Learns to Do More with Less after Losing 'Fair Share,'" *Indianapolis Star,* May 19, 1996.

39. Ibid.

40. "Judge's Ruling Goes Against IPS Teachers," *Indianapolis Star*, December 21, 1995.

41. "IPS and the Challenge of Privatization," *ISTA Advocate* (March–April 1995): 13.

42. "Senate Passes Education Bill Requiring Testing," *Indianapolis Star*, June 15, 2001.

43. "State Reforms Will Raise Bar for Schools," *Indianapolis Star*, June 20, 2001.

44. Indiana State Teachers Association, "Legislative Review, 1997 Session"; Conversation with Bob Margraf at his home in April 2001.

45. "ISTA Wields Big Stick in Legislature," *ISTA Advocate* XVII (October 1988): 3.

46. "ISTA: A Powerhouse in Statehouse," *Indianapolis Star*, February 7, 1988.

47. David J. Bodenhamer and Robert G. Barrows, eds., *The Encyclopedia of Indianapolis* (Bloomington: Indiana University Press, 1994), 1221; "ISTA's Role in Desegregation," *Teacher Advocate* II (April 1974): 6.

48. "Institutional Education: Facing a Phase-out?" *Teacher Advocate* II (April 1974): 8.

49. "ISTA Asks to Enter School Busing Suit," *Indianapolis News*, April 19, 1974.

50. "Indy Desegregation Continues," *Teacher Advocate* III (September 1974): 10.

51. "School Stays Denied, Intervention in Deseg OK'd," *Teacher Advocate* (September 1975): 10; "Indianapolis Desegregation Finally Begins," *Teacher Advocate* 8 (January–February 1980): 12.

Notes to Chapter XI

1. Dale Harris, Speech to ISTA Board of Directors, September 17, 1982.

2. "Advocate Interview: Warren Williams," *ISTA Advocate* XIII (March 1985): 5.

3. "Avoid Charges of Immorality or Misconduct," *ISTA Advocate* XIV (August 1985): 4.

4. Ibid.

5. "Interview: Williams," *ISTA Advocate* XIII (March 1985): 5; Warren Williams, oral history interview with Linda Weintraut, July 20, 2000.

6. Williams, interview with Weintraut.

7. Ibid.

8. "ISTA begins Construction of Addition," *ISTA Advocate* XVI (August 1987): 7; Williams, interview with Weintraut.

9. Robert Barcus, oral history interview with Weintraut and Warner, August 3, 2000; Williams, interview with Linda Weintraut.

10. Barcus, interview; Williams, interview with Weintraut.

11. Barcus, interview; Williams, interview with Weintraut.

12. Williams, interview with Weintraut; J. David Young, oral history interview with Linda Weintraut, July 18, 2000.

13. "ISTA Stakes out Own Insurance," *ISTA Advocate* XIV (March 1986): 9.

14. "ISTA Financial Services Corporation Offers Abundance of Benefits to Members," *ISTA Advocate* 27 (Fall 1997): 15.

15. Indiana State Teachers Association, *Financial Statements, 1998 and 1999*, 6, Indiana State Teachers Association Archives.

16. "Affirmative Action Plan of the Indiana State Teachers Association," *ISTA Handbook,* August 1999, Indiana State Teachers Association Archives.

17. "A New Vision for ISTA," *ISTA Advocate* 29 (Fall 1999): 4.

18. "ISTA Promotes Professional Development through Partnerships," *ISTA Advocate* 24 (November/December 1995): 8.

19. Indiana State Teachers Association, "Vision 2000: A Plan for the Future of the Indiana State Teachers Association," Spring 1994.

20. "What Is 'Professional,'" *ISTA Advocate* 27 (Spring 1998): 5.

21. "The Future of Bargaining and Bargaining the Future," *ISTA Advocate* 28 (Spring 1999): 5.

22. Young, interview.

23. Judith Briganti, interview with Linda Weintraut, November 13, 2001.

24. "O'Bannon Miscalculates on the Budget," *Indianapolis Star,* March 31, 2002; "Cutbacks Leave Teachers Without Helping Hands," *Indianapolis Star*, August 11, 2002.

Appendix I — Timeline

1854   George A. Chase, A. J. Vawter, E. P. Cole, Charles Barnes, Rev. E. Kent, and Caleb Mills, Indiana superintendent of public instruction, passed resolution to form a State Teacher's Association.

      Teachers' convention held on Monday, December 25, 1854, in College Hall at Indianapolis. Assembly adopted a constitution drafted by Caleb Mills. The next day, 150 new ISTA members met in the Capitol building and elected officers of the Association.

1855   First ISTA legislative committee worked with General Assembly on educational issues.

1856   First issue of *Indiana School Journal,* a refereed educational journal, published.

1861   Civil War began (ended in 1865).

1865   Indiana law made "upbraiding the teacher" by parents an offense with a maximum $25 fine.

      ISTA and the state superintendent supported schools for negroes on the grounds that education for all children benefited the state.

1870   ISTA constitution amended to require a nominating committee of one member from each congressional district in the state.

1873   First high school commissioned.

1874   By this year Abram C. Shortridge, Indianapolis superintendent, had established a 12-year school system with 3 divisions, primary, intermediate, and high school, with 4 grades in each.

1883   County superintendent created a committee to prepare lists of graduation examination questions.

1897   Compulsory school attendance law enacted for all children ages 7 to 14.

1898   The incoming president of ISTA, Francis M. Stalker, stated that teachers need a "closer organization" between regional teacher associations and ISTA.

1899   Act passed by Indiana General Assembly to consolidate hundreds of one-room schools.

1900   *Indiana School Journal* and *Inland Educator* merged into *The Educator—Journal.*

1905   General Assembly passed law that allowed the state superintendent to apportion 5.2 percent of school tax money, above the regular pupil apportionment, to poor school corporations.

1907   General Assembly passed laws for new professional requirements for teachers and trustees and ordered abandonment of schools with less than twelve students.

1908   In his address at ISTA's annual meeting Booker T. Washington "urged that the negro be kept in rural districts. . . . [For] in the tilling of the soil the negro received the best environment." He deplored especially the congregation of negroes in the Northern cities."

1910   ISTA sought passage of a law that provided "a disability benefit" for all teachers disabled after fifteen years of service in schools supported in full or part by state funds. Copies of the proposed bill were dispersed to all teachers to present to their representatives.

1913   "Women Teachers on the Warpath" announced a *News* headline. "Miss Beeson, a principal in Lafayette, and her educational suffragette forces" were demanding that the annual convention be moved from Christmas to October or November so the holidays could be spent with family.
        General Assembly passed first vocational education bill.

1914   Keynote speaker Dr. Charles Zueblin, Boston, said "when our teachers are paid as much as policemen and chauffeurs we will be able to get teachers to do all of this" work that is required of them.

1915   Anna Wilson, Crawfordsville, selected to be the second woman president of the association; the first woman president was Emma Mont. McRae.
        General Assembly passed first teachers' retirement law.

1916   Indiana State Federation of Public School Teachers, later ICTA, formed from local associations to defend rights of teachers.

1917   United States entered the Great War (war ended in 1918).

1918   Worldwide influenza pandemic struck, closing schools and forcing cancellation of annual ISTA convention.

1921   Contention at convention over amendment to the ISTA constitution that would reduce state convention to a small group of appointed delegates "who would have everything their own way."

1923   Teacher licensing law no longer called for county examinations for entry into the profession. The law required all new licenses and renewals be issued by the state board of education based on academic work completed at a teacher training institution.

1922   Charles O. Williams hired as first director.

1927   First teacher tenure law passed.

1929   Stock market crashed.

1933   General Assembly passed State School Relief Act, which provided more aid to poorer school corporations.

1935   Congress passed the "Little Red Rider," which forbade advocacy of or teaching about communism in the Washington, D.C., school system.

United States Congress passed the Social Security Act.

1938   Robert H. Wyatt became Executive Secretary.

1942   Resolutions committee recommended adoption of permanent platform that included statements on the rights of teachers to organize and responsibility for presenting all points of view in the classroom.

1945   Wyatt wrote legislation for reorganization of state board of education.

1947   ISTA called for an Indiana School Study Commission.

1949   Indiana School Study Commission report published.

ISTA elected an elementary school teacher as president for the first time.

1950   First Joint ISTA-ICTA Leadership Conference held at French Lick in August. Major issues were school legislation, school finance, public relations, and local associations.

Korean War began (armistice signed in 1953).

1951   Wyatt became chairman of NEA Legislative Commission.

ISTA chose new democratic Representative Assembly (RA) forum for annual conventions.

1953   ISTA RA adopted resolution against the "evils of communism."

1954   ISTA added a staff member to form a closer working relationship with the local associations of Indiana Classroom Teachers Association (ICTA).

ISTA celebrated 100th anniversary.

1955   Social Security added to teachers' pension plans.

1958   New ISTA building dedicated in October.

Indiana Retired Teachers Community, a newly formed corporation, announced plans for retired teachers home south of Greenwood, along US 31 in Johnson County. ISTA was not involved in financing the project but would assist in its management.

1959   School reorganization law passed.

ISTA sponsored Workshop on the Exceptional Child for elementary teachers during annual convention.

1960   Eleanor Roosevelt addressed the opening session of the annual convention.

1961   First collective bargaining bill for teachers enacted in Wisconsin.

1962   Wyatt elected president of the NEA.

1964   Dr. James B. Conant, former president of Harvard, charged that "public education in Indiana is ruled by an 'establishment' of professional educators."

1965   Wyatt urged a "Negotiation Bill for Teachers" to be presented to 1967 General Assembly to eliminate "the frustration and discouragement that pervades the decision-making process concerning teachers, [and] their compensation."

1966   ISTA adopted affiliation program, which automatically gave membership in ISTA to members of local teacher associations. This guaranteed ISTA direct access to the local affiliations and bypassed ICTA.

1967   ISTA established regional offices with field representatives who became a strong force in local bargaining (a forerunner of UniServ).

1968   First master contract was negotiated in Indiana between Highland School Board and the Highland Classroom Teachers Association.

1969   Indiana State Teachers Retirement Fund filed suit for fund money that was appropriated but not disbursed.

1970   Wyatt's title changed to executive director.

1971   Wyatt retired on April 30; Arnold W. Spilly became acting executive director until Ronald G. Jensen became executive director.

1972   Unification passed. Members of ISTA must also belong to the NEA and the local affiliate and vice versa.

        UniServ districts and staff positions established around the state.
        Indianapolis teachers strike.

1973   ICTA merged with ISTA.

        Public Law 217 passed.
        I-PACE formed.

1974   ISTA board of directors passed Association's first affirmative action plan for hiring and utilizing women and minorities in staff work within the organization and its affiliates.

1976   ISTA sent Joanna Hock, former president, to investigate conditions in the Warsaw schools after a series of vigilante raids into classrooms, public book-burnings, and discriminatory teacher firings.

        Six Marion teachers and two staff members jailed for strike after failure to reach contract agreement.

1978   Due process law for teachers passed.

1979   U.S. District Judge S. Hugh Dillin issued decision to desegregate Marion County schools by 1979–80 school year. Results in busing of 8,711 African American children to suburban schools. "This court does not consider that riding a reasonable distance . . . in a bus . . . imposes any burden upon the child thus transported."

1980   Jensen resigned effective January 1; Dale Harris became acting executive director (position later made permanent).

1983   Indiana Court of Appeals determined that "fair share" was modified form of "agency shop" and therefore legal. As a result, fair share could be included in collective bargaining agreements.

1984   State Board of Education reorganized to eliminate the three-committee system; now it was a single board of eleven members.

"Options Guaranteed," an automatic deduction of $12 a year earmarked to support pro-education candidates, passed the RA by a two to one margin. Provision also allowed members to cancel the deduction.

General Assembly passed bills for Prime Time and kindergarten.

1984   Dale E. Harris resigned; Vincent M. Kiernan became acting executive director.

1985   Warren Williams was hired as executive director.

1987   ISTA broke ground for addition to ISTA Center.

ISTEP passed this year and implemented in 1988 as part of Governor Orr's A+ Plan.

1988   ISTA Center dedicated after remodeling project.

A membership category of educational support pesonnel was created.

1992   Professional Standards Board established. This board governed teacher preparation and licensure.

ISTA-Retired, a memebership category of retired members, was created.

1995   ISTA promoted professional development through co-sponsorship of Goals 2000: Educate America Act.

1999 ISTA organized into six strategic teams: membership, member rights, legislative, political action, school quality, and public relations. Each team focused on development of strategic plans to implement ISTA governance.

2004 ISTA celebrated 150th anniversary.

Appendix II — ISTA Officers

Executive Directors

Charles O. Williams, 1924–1938

Robert H. Wyatt, 1938–1971

Arnold W. Spilly, 1971 (acting)

Ronald G. Jensen, 1971–1979

Dale E. Harris, 1980–1981 (acting)

Dale E. Harris, 1981–1984

Vincent M. Kiernan, 1984–1985 (acting)

Warren L. Williams, 1985–

Presidents

William M. Daily, 1854–1855

Charles Barnes, 1856

James G. May, 1857

Barnabas C. Hobbs, 1858

Caleb Mills, 1859

E. P. Cole, 1860

George A. Irvin, 1861

Cyrus Nutt, 1862

Allen R. Benton, 1863

Benjamin T. Hoyt, 1864

Ryland T. Brown, 1865

George Washington Hoss, 1866

Joseph F. Tuttle, 1867

Abram C. Shortridge, 1868

Joseph Tingley, 1869

David Eckley Hunter, 1870

A. M. Gow, 1871

William A. Bell, 1872

James H. Smart, 1873

William A. Jones, 1874

George P. Brown, 1875

William H. Wiley, 1876

J. H. Martin, 1877

John McKnight Bloss, 1878

J. T. Merrill, 1879

John Cooper, 1880

Hiram B. Jacobs, 1881

H. S. Tarbell, 1882

John S. Irwin, 1883

H. B. Hill, 1884

E. E. Smith, 1885

Cyrus W. Hodgin, 1886

Emma Mont. McRae, 1887

Lewis H. Jones, 1888

Jacob A. Zeller, 1889

William W. Parsons, 1890

Enoch A. Bryan, 1891

Justin N. Study, 1892

Lincoln O. Dale, 1893

Joseph Swain, 1894

Howard Sandison, 1895

James F. Scull, 1896

Robert A. Ogg, 1897

Francis M. Stalker, 1898

Will H. Glascock, 1899

Robert I. Hamilton, 1900

Henry B. Brown, 1901

Charles A. Prosser, 1902

Charles A. VanMatre, 1903

William Lowe Bryan, 1904

Edwin H. Hughes, 1905

Benjamin F. Moore, 1906

E. B. Bryan, 1907

George W. Benton, 1908

Robert J. Aley, 1909

Calvin N. Kendall, 1910

Samuel L. Scott, 1911

Charles A. Greathouse, 1912

A. O. Neal, 1913

Winthrop E. Stone, 1914

J. G. Collicott, 1915

Anna Wilson, 1916

George L. Roberts, 1917

No session, influenza, 1918

Horace Ellis, 1919

Clara L. Olcott, 1920

Donald DuShane, 1921

H. L. Smith, 1922

Elsa Huebner Olson, 1923

Benjamin Burris, 1924

William P. Dearing, 1925

Martha A. Whitacre, 1926

C. W. Goucher, 1927

C. E. Hinshaw, 1928

Ralph N. Tirey, 1929

Mattie B. Fry, 1930

Milo H. Stuart, 1931

Clara Rathfon, 1932

Robert B. Hougham, 1933

L. V. Phillips, 1934

Albert Free, 1935

Hilda Maehling, 1936

Wendell Wright, 1937

Rose E. Boggs, 1938

K. V. Ammerman, 1939

Margaret Sweeney, 1940

J. Fred Hull, 1941

Sara W. Ewing, 1942

H. B. Allman, 1943

Virginia Kinnaird, 1944

L. T. Buck, 1945

Anita Oldham, 1946

W. E. Wilson, 1947

Gertrude E. McComb, 1948

R. E. Hood, 1949

Thelma Ballard, 1950

H. E. Binford, 1951

Eleanor Bly, 1952

George Ostheimer, 1953

Mary Van Horn, 1954

Glade Rohrer, 1955

Rhoda Williams, 1956

O. M. Swihart, 1957

Audrey Shauer, 1958

Earl A. Johnson, 1959

Blanche Penrod, 1960

Henry L. McHargue, 1961

Sparkle Crowe, 1962

Glen Barkes, 1963

Helen Blackledge, 1964

C. Edgar Stahl, 1965

Nell Bethel, 1966

Charles L. Sharp, 1967

Thelma Spannbauer, 1968

Charles T. Reece, 1969

Louella T. Martin, 1970

Ernest W. Horn, 1971

Joanna Hock, 1972–1973

James Hirschinger, 1974

Raymond A. Gran, 1975–1977

Cordell Affeldt, 1977–1982

Damon P. Moore, 1983–1988

Garrett L. Harbron, 1989–1994

J. David Young, 1995–2001

Judith Briganti, 2002–

Bibliography

Books

Baker, William C. *Pride and Progress: The Story of the Louisiana Teachers Association.* Washington, D.C.: National Education Association, 1989.

Blumenfeld, Samuel L. *NEA Trojan Horse in American Education.* Boise, Idaho: Paradigm Company, 1984.

Bodenhamer, David J., and Robert G. Barrows, eds. *The Encyclopedia of Indianapolis.* Bloomington: Indiana University Press, 1994.

Brinkley, Alan. *Unfinished Nation: A Concise History of the American People.* Volume 2. New York: McGraw Hill, 1993.

Butler, Susan Lowell. *The National Education Association: A Special Mission.* New York: NEA, 1987.

Carmony, Donald F. *Indiana, 1816–1850: The Pioneer Era.* Indianapolis: Indiana Historical Society, 1998.

Comer, Fred R. *Coming of Age: Teachers in Iowa 1954 to 1993.* Des Moines: Iowa State Education Association, 1993.

Gitlin, Todd. *The Sixties: Years of Hope, Days of Rage.* New York: Bantam, 1987.

Gray, Jerome A., Joe L. Reed, and Norman W. Walton. *History of the Alabama State Teachers Association.* Washington, D.C.: National Education Association, 1987.

Halberstam, David. *The Fifties.* New York: Fawcett Columbine, 1993.

Heale, M. J. *American AntiCommunism: Combating the Enemy Within, 1830–1970.* Baltimore, MD: The Johns Hopkins University Press, 1990.

Katz, Michael B. *In the Shadow of the Poorhouse: A Social History of Welfare in America.* New York: Basic Books, 1996.

Macleod, David I. *The Age of the Child: Children in America, 1890–1920.* New York: Simon & Schuster, Inc., 1998.

Madison, James H. *Indiana Through Tradition and Change: A History of the Hoosier State and Its People.* Indianapolis: Indiana Historical Society, 1982.

————. *The Indiana Way: A State History.* Indianapolis: Indiana Historical Society and Indiana University Press, 1986.

Matusow, Alan J. *The Unraveling of America: A History of Liberalism in the 1960s.* New York: Harper & Row Publishers, 1984.

Miller, James. *Democracy Is in the Streets: From Port Huron to the Siege of Chicago.* New York: Simon & Schuster, Inc., 1989.

Moores, Charles W. *Caleb Mills and Indiana School System.* Indianapolis: Indiana Historical Society, 1905.

National Education Association. *Separating the Wheat from the Chaff: How Much Do Schools Really Benefit When States Raise Taxes on Their Behalf?* Washington, D.C.: NEA, 1996.

Pears, Thomas Clinton, Jr., *New Harmony: An Adventure in Happiness, Papers of Thomas and Sarah Pears.* Indianapolis: Indiana Historical Society, 1933.

Phillips, J. Clifton. *Indiana in Transition: The Emergence of an Industrial Commonwealth, 1880–1920.* Indianapolis: Indiana Historical Bureau and Indiana Historical Society, 1968.

Riley, Glenda. *Divorce: An American Tradition.* New York: Oxford University Press, 1991.

Skopol, Theda. *Protecting Soldiers and Mothers: The Political Origins of Social Policy in the United States.* Cambridge: The Belknap Press of Harvard University Press, 1992.

Thornbrough, Emma Lou. *Indiana in the Civil War Period 1850–1880.* Indianapolis: Indiana Historical Bureau and Indiana Historical Society, 1965.

Tindall, George Brown. *America: A Narrative History.* Volume 1. New York: W.W. Norton & Company, 1992.

Urban, Wayne J. *More than the Facts: The Research Division of the National Education Association 1922–1997.* New York: University Press of America, Inc., 1998.

Walsh, Justin E. *The Centennial History of the Indiana General Assembly 1816–1978.* Indianapolis: Indiana Historical Bureau, 1987.

Zilversmit, Arthur. *Changing Schools: Progressive Education Theory and Practice, 1930–1960.* Chicago: University of Chicago Press, 1993.

Periodicals

Adams, L. M. Campbell. "An Investigation of Housing and Living Conditions in Three Districts in Indianapolis." *Indiana University Studies* 8, no. 3 (September 1910).

Lynch, William O. "The Great Awakening." *Indiana Magazine of History* 41 (1945): 108.

Morris, Joe Alex. "They Don't Want Uncle's Money." *Saturday Evening Post,* 22 March 1952: 30–31, 141–42, 144.

Robinson, Robert B., and Ana-Maria Wahl. "Industrial Employment and Wages of Women, Men, and Children in a 19th Century City: Indianapolis, 1850–1880." *American Sociological Review* 55 (December 1990): 912–28.

Government Documents

State of Indiana, Department of Public Instruction, *19th Biennial Report of the State Superintendent* (31 July 1897–31 July 1898).

State of Indiana, "Report of the Committee on Education," *Common School Report 1843–51.*

State of Indiana, *Acts of 1991, 107th Indiana General Assembly.* Volume 3. 1991.

State of Indiana, Indiana Education Survey Commission. *Public Education in Indiana.* New York: General Education Commission, 1923.

State of Indiana. *Laws of the State of Indiana,* 1943.

United States Government. *Decennial Census of the United States- 1840.*

United States Government. *Decennial Census of the United States- 1850.*

Indiana State Teachers Association Documents/Publications

Indiana State Teachers Association. *Collective Bargaining Law 25th Year Commemorative, 1998.*

Indiana State Teachers Association. *Proceedings of the Representative Assembly.* October 1973 and May 1974.

Indiana State Teachers Association. "Memorial in Retrospect." No date.

Indiana State Teachers Association. *Financial Statements, 1998 and 1999.*

Indiana State Teachers Association. "Various Public Education Programs Enacted and Funded by the Indiana General Assembly," July 1, 1983– June 30, 1997.

Indiana State Teachers Association. *Indiana State Teachers Association Handbook,* 1970, 1971, 1975–76.

Indiana State Teachers Association. *Budgets of the Indiana State Teachers Association.* 1976–88.

Indiana State Teachers Association. "Affirmative Action Plan of the Indiana State Teachers Association." *ISTA Handbook.* August 1999.

Indiana School Journal 1856–66; 1870–76; 1896

The Inland Educator 1898

The Educator Journal 1909–10

The Indiana Teacher 1924–35; 1944–49; 1950–57; 1970

Teacher Advocate 1973–75

ISTA Advocate 1981–97

Newspapers

Bedford Daily Times-Mail

Columbia City Commercial Mail

Elkhart Truth

Elwood Call

Indianapolis Journal

Indianapolis News

Indianapolis Star

Indianapolis Times

Louisville Courier Journal

Monticello Herald-Tribune

Muncie Star

Richmond Palladium-Item

Oral History Interviews

Barcus, Robert. Oral History Interview with Linda Weintraut and John Warner, August 3, 2000.

Borgman, Sarah. Oral History Interview with Linda Weintraut, July 28, 2000.

Margraf, Robert. Oral History Interview with John Warner, July 14, 2000 and September 21, 2000.

Moore, Damon. Oral History Interview with John Warner, July 27, 2000.

Ransford, John. Oral History Interview with John Warner, July 27, 2000.

Williams, Warren. Oral History Interview with Linda Weintraut, July 20, 2000.

Wyatt, Robert Hall. Interview by Randell W. Jehs, Indiana State Library Oral History Project (1972–75): 1–3.

Young, J. David. Oral History Interview with Linda Weintraut, July 18, 2000.

Unpublished Material

Collins, Warren F. "A History of the Indiana State Teachers' Association." MA Thesis, Indiana University, 1926.

———. "History of the Indiana State Federation of Public School Teachers." 1951.

Letter, October 1917, Correspondence, vol. 13, Indiana State Council of Defense, ISA.

Weintraut, Linda. "The Limits of 'Enlightened Self-Interest': Business Power in Indianapolis." Ph.D. diss., Indiana University, 2001.

Miscellaneous

Indiana Department of Public Instruction Study. *Why Does Indiana Rank 17?* 1920.

Speech by Robert H. Wyatt, May 10, 1973. Indiana State Teachers Association, Indianapolis, Indiana.

Board of Trustees of the Retirement Fund. "Indiana State Teachers' Retirement Fund.

Bulletin of Information Regarding the Retirement Law, As Amended by the Law of 1937–1939." 1940.

Good, Lara P. "Teachers' Contract," Blackford County, Indiana. 1914.

Hock, Joanna. Response to questionnaire. 2000.

"Our ISTA at 140 Years." Remarks to Representative Assembly by Garrett L. Harbron, October 22, 1994.

Dale Harris, Speech to ISTA Board of Directors, September 17, 1982.

Index